Confidence - Anxiety Script
Pre-talk & Hypnosis
Psychotherapy
& Hypnotherapy
Neuro-Linguistic Programming (NLP)
Cognitive Behavioural Therapy (CBT)
Clinical Psychology

By
David Glenn

I am dedicating this book to my clients, in appreciation.
Thank you, because without you I would never have had the experience,
and therefore the knowledge, to write this book.
David Glenn.

Disclaimer, Legal Warning and Notice

The CD Rom that is mentioned in this book is given to those studying as a Diploma with me personally. It is not given out for free with this book.

☐

Contents

Introduction

THOSE STUDENTS THAT HAVE READ MY BOOK: "Beginner to Advanced Practitioner Training Course & Self Development in Psychotherapy - Hypnotherapy - Neuro-Linguistic Programming (NLP) - Cognitive Behavioural Therapy (CBT)

Client Psychology Volume One", will not need to read this book. The information within this book has already been covered in the book just mentioned. Even so, I have also published this script as a separate digital book for those people that requested me to do so.

This book is more than just a confidence script. I will share with you many examples of real clients that I treated in therapy. The examples are: anxiety, depression, stress, jealousy, low confidence, sport athletes, and even anger management. I will show you how I structure a set plan for a therapy session, and of what needs to be done to help the client overcome their problem. Also I will explain to you the knowledge that the client needs to be educated on, in order to help them further. Even though I have a set plan, please remember to always personalise a session to the client within the plan.

The script in this book has been written in a way, not intended to be read out to the clients, word for word. I simply want to show you different beginners and advanced ways of conducting therapy, in a structured session that you can personalise to each client. This script can be adapted to help clients with anxiety, depression, stress, jealousy, low confidence and even anger management. I have written both the pre-talk and what is said under hypnosis to the client far longer than it need be. I have done this purposely, to give you more examples of what can be said, so that you can pick and choose what you feel fits that particular client best. So, once again, please note that this script is not intended to be read word for word to the client. It can even be used in a number of sessions, if needed, to make each session different from the previous.

I am David Glenn, a Professional Psychotherapist, Hypnotherapist, NLP Practitioner and Trainer with over twenty year's experience in this profession. I have written this book to pass on my knowledge for those:

1) Interested in the cognitive psychology of oneself as a self-development help guide in understanding and utilising the power of your own mind to overcome: Low confidence and anxiety in order to get the best out of your life.

2) Wanting to have a successful career in Hypnotherapy, Neuro-Linguistic Programming (NLP), Cognitive Behavioural Therapy (CBT), Life Coaching and Psychotherapy as a whole. Developing or enhancing your therapy skills in dealing with low self-esteem clients, to help them recover their cognitive health and wellbeing.

Everybody can study this script course book as home study training. It is laid out in layman's terms, so those with no previous knowledge of the subject, can still learn how to use the power of your own mind to enrich your life. Even if you do not want to be a Professional Therapist, you can still study this course to understand yourself more, for self-help and personal development. This will enable you to break negative habits, and have unlimited confidence with the techniques that you can learn and use in your life, or therapy practice to improve your psyche, or that of a client's cognitive health (psychological health) and wellbeing. You will also learn how to hypnotise your clients, friends and family, and find the beneficial power of self-hypnosis.

Enrich your knowledge and skills with what I am going to teach you, which can be used in general life, for yourself and others, or by those wishing a new profession in Hypnotherapy, CBT, NLP Practitioner or Psychotherapist. Keep an open mind to new possibilities. How you have thought, communicated, and acted throughout life, may need to change, or be adapted for positive effect. I will teach you the tools of how this can be done to enable you or others to move on positively in life.

Once you have read and fully understood this book, for many people it is a life changing experience. My philosophy on therapy and psychology in general is - it is the art of understanding the psychology of people, our behaviour, the mind model, body language, communication and speech. You will be able to understand how your mind works, and how to utilise its power for positive change.

Anyone on earth, if able bodied, can drive, or learn to drive a car. Be that as it may, that does not mean you will ever be a professional rally, or formula one racing car driver. In order to be the formula one expert in the psychotherapy world, you have to have that special something: innate quality. You cannot think, act, or communicate as the general public do. In general life, what you think is rude, morally wrong, or what you would not dream of saying to a fellow human being in public, those same rules do not apply in the therapy room, because the client is paying you for a highly skilled service. You must never allow your own personality to effect what needs to be done, in order to help the client progress forwards positively in their lives. Conducting therapy is not about you or your beliefs; it is about what is best for the client, even if you have to be cruel to be kind, and go outside of your comfort zone. You may have thought that therapy is just about counselling, empathy, listening, understanding, relating to, comforting and simply relaxing a person. It is far more complex than that. You are not there to comfort a client; you are there to enable them to become unstuck, get out from their negative mindset, and move forward for positive effect and self-fulfilment. You are there to enable them to see the wood from the trees, so they can find the truth about themselves. Thereby you can support them with education, by imparting psychotherapy knowledge that can be adapted, to enable growth and movement. You will understand this more as you learn, by reading through this book in full.

I have met many students that have all the knowledge they require to be great Hypnotherapist, CBT, NLP Therapists, but yet many lack intuition. This is a skill that you either already have, or you have not. Without it, success as a psychotherapist will be limited. Of course I have also met many students that have no confidence whatsoever, and I watch them grow and develop into great therapists through the knowledge from my training.

I have a very modern approach to therapy for today's generation, as I am sure you will come to realise as we continue. Once you have absorbed all the knowledge I am about to teach you, you will know more than most therapists that have been in the profession for many years. This book contains valuable information on becoming a Professional Hypnotherapist, and Psychotherapist, despite that I still advise all my students to practise on volunteers, for charities, family and friends, before their first paying client. Conducting psychotherapy is an extremely complex and skilful job. Therefore after reading this book, and gaining some practical skills, if you do not feel you have the ability to put in place the knowledge I have imparted in this book, then I will teach you the skills in a group or one on one setting. Through tailor-made training this will enable you to set up in business, with the greatest confidence in knowledge and skills to succeed in a successful psychotherapy career.

Prepare yourself for a truly amazing, life-changing experience. Enjoy as you learn, and I guarantee, at times you will be thinking: WOW! MIND BLOWING, INSPIRATIONAL KNOWLEDGE AND WISDOM, ALL IN THIS BOOK!

My recommendation is to read this book, in its entirety, more than once, to fully understand the connection between each skill being taught. Please do not speed read this book, or skip chapters. Take your time to absorb all the information being taught.

It will also be most beneficial to put the knowledge and skills into practise, by attending my group training workshop sessions or one to one training.

The Workings of the Mind Model Bulletin Points

AS A STUDENT, before you conduct a therapy session with any type of client, you first must learn the mind model and memorise it. I have added the bulletin points of the Mind Model in this chapter to help you.

Three parts of the whole mind:

1) Conscious Mind Functions: Rational logical thought - Makes decisions, but the subconscious determines on whether those decisions are carried out or not - One task at once - Willpower - General speech.

2) Subconscious Mind Functions: Many tasks at once - Memories - Imagination - Emotions - Habits - Protects us - In control - Intelligence - Perception of reality - Habitual speech.

3) Analytical or Critical Area: This part of the mind is the conduit connection between the conscious and subconscious, passing information between the two main parts of the whole mind. It is the part of the mind that reasons to determine new information as being

fact or fiction (real or fake), based on information from the subconscious memories.

The subconscious four reference points:

(A) The subconscious mind does not know the difference between what is real or imagined.
(B) The subconscious also does not know the difference between good habits, or bad habits. A habit is a habit through repetition regardless.
(C) The subconscious has no concept of time, past, present or future with regards to associated links.
(D) The subconscious also works via associated links, which are memories, cognitive thought (a persons perception of fact or fiction, real or fake, true or false-truth), and emotions (pain or pleasure), that are associated (connected), within the mind to an anchor. This can be any sound, touch, taste, smell, or seeing a certain person (or behaviour), colour, object or place.

The seven mind rules:

1) Ideas or thoughts result in physical immediate emotional reactions.
2) The subconscious mind delivers what we focus on.
3) Repeated negative or positive focused thoughts result in long-term organic change over time.
4) Imagination overpowers knowledge within in the mind.
5) Fixed thoughts can only be replaced by another via the subconscious.
6) Opposing ideas cannot be held at the same time.
7) Conscious effort alone, results in opposite subconscious success.

Seven Important Mind Rules

MOST PEOPLE WRONGLY BELIEVE that the mind and body are two separate things, but the brain is part of the body as a whole, and the mind is part of the brain. You are one being, so the mind and body are the same whole, because they are connected.

One: Ideas or thoughts result in physical immediate emotional reactions - Thought processes affect the reactions of your immediate behaviour, even if you are not consciously aware of your reaction. For example, a micro-signal in the facial area of looking upset. Negative thoughts of any kind develop instantly into negative, physical, emotional changes within the body. Example: blushing, or imagining being upset, or crying in a certain situation, will result in you doing so, by just the thought of being confronted by that situation. If you imagine a spider is going to hurt you, then the imagined idea causes a physical, emotional, negative reaction to fear, even though the spider is of no danger to you and may not even be there. Thoughts that release powerful emotions, whether real or imagined will, without fail, seep into subconscious mind. Physical, emotional reactions then occur, due to the subconscious accepting the negative thoughts as fact. This is due to the subconscious mind not knowing the difference between what is real or imagined. Of course happy thoughts also have an instant effect on your emotions, and therefore your body as well, by having a positive effect on the body unlike negative thoughts. Consider the mind and body as being the same thing, because the mind is part of the body, therefore whatever thought you have, affects every living cell within your body, either negatively or positively, depending on your thought, so it's best to think positively.

Two: The subconscious mind delivers what we focus on - When wanting to achieve a realistic goal that you are not already doing, if you focus your subconscious mind on a negative, then a negative result is what will be achieved and the goal is failed. Alternatively, by playing a positive movie of achieving that same goal within your imagination, then you will achieve that goal on a conscious level, because your subconscious mind believes you have already achieved it, and that makes it easier to do so via the subconscious auto pilot. The reason the subconscious believes you have already achieved the goal, is because you played the positive movie of doing so, and the subconscious mind does not know the difference between what is real or imagined, because both are your reality. You made a conscious decision to do something, your subconscious then plays a positive movie of what you consciously want to achieve, and by doing so, it makes a task easier to achieve, due to the two parts of the mind working in agreement, instead of being in conflict.

What I have just written above, is in relation to a person that wants to achieve a goal that they should be doing, but are not doing it. However, a person with a bad habit is the opposite, because they are already doing something that they should not be doing, so the focus of the subconscious mind has to be different. A person with a bad habit wrongly focuses the subconscious mind with the association of pleasure to the habit, this positive association must be changed to a negative focused association, in order to stop the bad habit. We are often asked, "Who are you?" The simple answer is to tell the questioner your name. However, that does not really tell them who you are. The real answer is, "I am what I focus my subconscious mind on."

Three: Repeated negative or positive focused thoughts result in long-term organic change over time - When ill, negative, repeated, focused thoughts you have about yourself delay the healing process, and can even kill you with stress due to causing heart failure. When positive with uplifting thoughts, we tend to recover faster from illness. This is the mind and body connection being the same thing. A large percentage of human illnesses are functional as opposed to organic, so continued, negative, focused thoughts that you have about yourself, result in long-term, organic, negative change and therefore illness. The term used is "Psychosomatic" (illness caused by the mind).So, mind rule one and two develops into mind rule three, if the person continues the negative thoughts about them self. People that cause illness through the mind can be classed as neurotic, and the term used for a person that continuously has psychosomatic illness is a hypochondriac. Even though some people have genuine diseases, negative, repeated, focused thoughts will still result in further negative long-term organic change over time. With the use of hypnosis, the effect from the negative, focused thought can be changed, by changing the thought to positive. Be that as it may, a negative thought can also result in positive, organic change. For example: a negative thought towards the bad habit of smoking, means the organic change is better for long-term health due to the client avoiding smoking. Of course positive focused thoughts result in long-term positive health benefits for the mind and body.

Four: Imagination overpowers knowledge within in the mind - A smoker has the conscious knowledge that smoking is killing them, but yet they have not imagined the negative effects within the subconscious mind. The subconscious mind is therefore still playing a positive, imagined, associated movie toward the bad habit, and therefore the person does not change, because imagination has overpowered their knowledge, even though the positive association to the habit is wrong and is killing them. Once again remember that imagination (subconscious mind), is more powerful than knowledge (conscious mind), and the subconscious always wins, even when wrong. In order to do anything in life, you have to first imagine doing it, hence why imagination (subconscious mind), is more powerful than knowledge (conscious mind), within the whole mind. This is why people fail, they have made a conscious decision for change, and then tried to consciously succeed, but it is impossible to consciously stop smoking, lose weight, or any bad habit, when the subconscious is still playing a positive movie towards the bad habit. Change the positive to a negative within the subconscious and the bad habit is avoided. With regards to people with depression, anxiety, stress, low confidence etc, the movie within their subconscious is of wrongly believing an imagined, negative thought as fact. Example: a person may imagine that it is fact that they are useless, ugly etc, so they feel depressed and fear, even though they are wrong, but the negative, imagined thought is fact in their warped perception of reality. Change the imagined thought to agree with logic knowledge, and the person's reality changes for the positive and the problem is solved.

Five: Fixed thoughts can only be replaced by another via the subconscious - If every morning at 7am I got up and consciously made the decision to tap my head three times with my hand, the subconscious, eventually through repetition, takes the task on as a habit, it has become a fixed thought and it is incorporated into my morning ritual. This habit would then be protected by the subconscious. So to get up one morning and consciously force myself not to tap my head, would result in an overwhelming urge of anxiety, as if something is wrong, as if there is a potential danger. This anxiety of feeling there is a danger, is simply the subconscious mind reminding me to do the habit, because it wrongly feels it is doing me a favour protecting that habit, by keeping me from harm.

In order to overcome this anxiety, and to stop a potential danger, be it real or not, the subconscious reminds me of the habit, so I tap my head for instant relief from anxiety. In other words there is a subconscious resistance to change because the subconscious mind believes it is doing me a favour, so continues to protect the habit even though it is not healthy to do so. Remember the subconscious does not know the difference between a good or bad habit, it protects it regardless, as if there is a danger not to do so. It is simply an associated link between getting up in the morning and tapping my head that became a habit. In other words, repetition that has become a habit through an associated link. Changing the associated link subconsciously, will bring about permanent results.

For example, imagining myself getting up in the morning and doing press-ups, this would occupy my hands so as not to tap my head, and over time the press-ups become a new more positive habit. This is why a smoker always wants a cigarette first thing in the morning, due to the association of waking up and smoking, they have never imagined doing something else and not smoking.

Dear student, as far as the subconscious mind is concerned, what is the difference between the habit of smoking and the habit of me tapping my head? Think about that for a moment.

The answer is no difference, because both habits are protected within the subconscious, both create anxiety if not carried out, they are in fact the same. A habit. So now let me ask, what is the difference between smoking and swimming within the subconscious? The answer is they are the same, because both habits are protected, because the subconscious mind does not know the difference between swimming and smoking, both are a habit regardless of them being good or bad. The habit of swimming is protected to stop you from the danger of drowning if you fall in to a river, and the habit of smoking is protected to save you from potential danger that's not real. Your subconscious doesn't know there is no danger by not smoking, because the smoker has never told the subconscious mind of the danger of doing the habit in the first place. They have associated pleasure to it, so of course they keep smoking. The fixed thought that needs to be changed, needs to be replaced via the subconscious, because that is where the habit is stored, and not in the conscious mind, so of course consciously wanting to change will always result in failure, due to mind rule four: "Imagination overpowers knowledge within in the mind", and a combination of the other mind rules. You are starting to see how these seven mind rules are all connected, and of course they are, because we only have one mind each.

Six: Opposing ideas cannot be held at the same time - This means that once the subconscious has accepted an idea as fact, then any opposing conscious ideas will always be rejected. The subconscious, always conflicts against an opposing idea from the conscious mind, and as you know the subconscious is the stronger part of the mind and therefore, overpowers the opposing conscious idea or thought. That is true unless you change an idea on a subconscious level so that both parts of the mind are in agreement. For example: a person consciously thinks "I want to stop smoking", but they continue to smoke because their subconscious is protecting the habit and positive associated links of smoking, due to them not showing their subconscious any differently. Remember mind rule four: "Imagination overpowers knowledge within in the mind", which means the subconscious overpowers the conscious, and that of course has a detrimental effect on a person's life, and that is why, in order to change, it has to be done subconsciously first, to then be a conscious act. Also the subconscious cannot have two opposing ideas at the same time, for example: it cannot think fact (real) and fiction (not real), towards an idea at the same time, it is one or the other idea. The same with the conscious mind, you cannot logically think something is true and false at the same time. Nonetheless as you now know, the conscious can try to oppose an idea from the subconscious, but again, two opposing ideas cannot be held at the same time, so the stronger more powerful subconscious wins.

Seven: Conscious effort alone, results in opposite subconscious success - Conscious effort alone, results in opposite, subconscious success, means that; if you only consciously attempt to try and achieve your goal, you will fail every time. For example: a weight loss client consciously thinks, "I don't want that chocolate bar because I don't need it. " They have, by doing so, implanted within the subconscious mind, an image of them wanting it and eating it, the exact opposite of the conscious thought. So the client then eats the chocolate due to the powerful suggestion of the image in their subconscious mind of doing so. If you say to yourself consciously "Don't think of a black cat", then subconsciously you have thought of one, the opposite of what you wanted to achieve. This is why conscious effort alone will never work to overcome a problem, and as you now know, the subconscious is more powerful than the conscious, and it overpowers the conscious will every time. This is why hypnosis is so successful in helping people overcome any problem.

Successfully Boosting Confidence Session Explained

SUCCESSFULLY OVERCOMING anxiety, depression, stress sessions etc, are broken down into three parts:

a) Pre-talk
b) Suggestibility test
c) Hypnosis session

This script can be adapted to help clients with anxiety, depression, stress, jealousy, low confidence and even anger management. After reading the phobia script book and then this one, you will realise that low confidence is very similar to a phobia, and can be treated in the same way in some cases. So what is the difference between a phobia and nervousness or low confidence? The emotions are almost the same as they produce the same negative reaction, but the extremes are different in each client type. The difference between them is that, before a session, a person with a phobia never confronts their fear because the reaction would be extreme, and a person with low confidence still confronts the thing they have anxiety with, even if at a limited function. You can use parts of this script and the phobia script to help your clients by adapting the scripts to suit the individual person. You will also come to realise as we continue, that in some cases, the emotion of: "Nerves" is almost the same as the build up of excitement before an event, the two (nerves and excitement), can be confused within your client's mind for one or the other.

Examples of Real Boosting Confidence and Overcoming Anxiety Clients

Before I explain the pre-talk, I will give you some examples of clients that I have treated successfully.

I booked a male client in for a session, and previous to the session he could not urinate in public toilets due to convincing himself that he was being watched, which caused him to feel nervous anxiety. This is a very common reaction with men in public toilets. This is a nervous reaction that he had created in his own mind, which is similar to a phobia, but not as extreme, because he was confronting his fear, even though he had failed to overcome the nervous tension. Even if no one else was in the toilet area he would worry that someone would walk in on him at the urinal, and this prevented him from urinating. Obviously this was his imagination creating the: "Fright, Fight or Flight Responses," due to the habit.

He would go to a football match and at half time when everyone else was going to the toilet he would hold it in and wait until the start of the second half, before going to the toilet. He did that because he knew that everyone else would once again be watching the match, having finished in the toilet so, he would have the place to himself. So this problem was affecting his enjoyment of football, and life in general, a very serious problem for him. In the pre-talk, I discovered that he was a businessman that had never failed in a new business venture, so I expanded on that information and via hypnosis, I associated the act of urinating to the feeling of building up a new business, so that if he didn't urinate the new business would fail. This drove him to succeed because he was a man that got great pleasure from success of business, and this new business of urinating was no different to any other new business that I had created within his subconscious mind. Adding to the thought of urinating to being a new business, I also took other information he had given me in the pre-talk, that being that he is comfortable going to the toilet in front of his girlfriend, and so I used that information whilst he was under hypnosis by playing the movie within his subconscious that anyone that came into the toilet area was a copy of his girlfriend. Remember that the subconscious mind doesn't know the difference between what's real or imagined so this was very successful for him. Added to this, I gave him a confidence boost session as explained later in this book. A week later he emailed me to thank me, because he had overcome his past problem.

Staying with the theme of urinating, one male client became very anxious when in public buildings if he could not see a toilet door, or if he didn't know where the nearest toilet was within the building. He had convinced himself that if the doorway to a toilet could not be seen, then he would not get there in time if he needed the toilet. If people were standing and chatting in front of a toilet door, then he saw this as an obstacle or wall that he could not get past. This made him very anxious, because he thought those people would block the door way and not move if he needed to go to the toilet. Therefore, in his mind, he thought he would urinate in his trousers, even though that had never happened, so it was all in his imagination and imagination overpowers knowledge within the mind as a whole. He had the knowledge of it never happening, but yet still imagined that it would. On entering any new building, the first thing he would do was walk around to locate the toilets and plan a route in his mind from where he was going to be, to the toilet. He was going to an office works party soon and the thought was causing him stress, because the event was being held in an unfamiliar building, so he did not know where the toilets were. I started the session as I would any confidence session, as shown later.

I then had to make him see how ridiculous his thoughts were, so, under hypnosis I played the movie in his mind that he was chatting to his boss in a room full of people at the party. To the left of his boss was a toilet door, with people standing between his boss and the toilet door. Instead of playing the movie with my client wanting the toilet, I played it so that it was his boss. I did this so as not to cause any unnecessary anxiety in my client's mind and so he was made aware that the imagined situation was not happening to him, meaning he was an observer. Plus, by using his boss in the imagined scenario, it made the event that was about to happen in my client's mind, look more ridiculous and I was ridiculing the situation and not the client. In this imagined scenario I made the client witness his boss say that he needed the toilet and so his boss excused himself from the conversation. Of course I was playing the part of his boss when saying: "It's nice talking with you, but please excuse me as I need the toilet." The other guests heard this, and decided that they would form a line of people to block the door to the toilets to prevent the boss from entering the toilet area. People were pushing and holding his boss back from the door preventing him from getting to the toilet whilst they laughed at him, and they also pulled his trousers down waiting for him to urinate.

By doing this I was making the situation humorous and ridiculous at the same time, so as to change my client's way of thinking. I wanted him to realise that this situation that he had been stressed about all these years, would never really happen to him. My client started to laugh whilst he was still hypnotised, so I knew he had changed his thoughts on that situation. However, he surprised me after the session by asking me in a very serious way why I had humiliated his boss like that. Clearly he was confused by not yet being fully conscious from the trance state. I had to explain that I had not embarrassed his boss, because what he had witnessed in his mind had only happened within his mind and his boss would never have known about it because it wasn't real. This is a good example of how the subconscious mind cannot tell the difference between what is imagined or what is real, and so my client thought it had really happened. He started to fully awaken from trance and then his logical mind (conscious) realised it wasn't real and why I had used his boss in the scenario and not him. He thanked me because the session was successful.

The original event-cause of this man's problem was simply that he was previously in a staff meeting at work and he felt that he needed to go to the toilet. He already felt a little anxious due to being in the meeting, and this negative feeling escalated with the thought of stopping the meeting to having to walk past everyone by leaving the room to go to the toilet. However he couldn't handle that thought, so he remained in the meeting because he felt it would be embarrassing to leave with everyone knowing he needed the toilet. He didn't want all the attention from people watching him leave the room, because to him, that was humiliating, which created more anxiety, so he remained sat in the meeting and the anxiety then built up with the added discomfort of the thought of wanting to urinate.

This is a good example of how a person can reassociate an emotion. This man was nervous in a works meeting which caused the: "Fright Response," which made him think he needed the toilet when the likelihood is that he didn't need to go to the toilet at all. So the emotion he was feeling from nervous tension from being in a meeting was reassociated to the anchor, within his subconscious mind of focusing on the thought of needing to urinate with the wrong thought that he was being prevented from doing so. Of course his thought process was irrational because I am sure people wouldn't have given it much thought if he had left the room and they would have carried on with the meeting. His subconscious wrongly assumed that the people in the room were preventing him from going to the toilet, when in fact he was preventing himself, with the imagined thought of the reaction from the people in the room. His imagination takes over and he sees the people as a barrier in preventing him from going to the toilet. Basically what was initially a simple feeling of nervousness in a works meeting caused the: "Fright Response," which escalated the nervousness because when a person is in: "Fright," their bladder opens because it is not needed in fright. Be that as it may, I know he did not need to urinate because if he did then he would have wet himself, the fact that he didn't means it was just a state of mind that he lost control over. The escalated nervous anxiety within his subconscious mind was associated to the anchor and stored within his subconscious to be reactivated in the future, should he need the toilet in a place of work. Obviously the anchor was the feeling of needing to go to the toilet, and the association being the thought of anxiety of being blocked or prevented from going by other people, so he feared wetting himself in the work place. If this client had not received help when he did, then this anxiety disorder would have defiantly developed in to a phobia of the thought of going to the toilet at work or even in public places. He would have then avoided all public or work toilets, which would have made daily life very difficult.

Another male client thought he lacked confidence when riding his motorbike in dirt bike racing competitions. He would get so worked up and anxious before a race that he would vomit. You will find this happens to a lot of sports people, from boxers, golfers to runners etc, but they are unknowingly simply confusing their emotions. My client loved dirt bike racing, it was his first love and once the race began he would feel fine and confident, and he really enjoyed it. So, he could not understand why, as he perceived it, that he had the negative reaction before each race. He did have confidence during the race and he continued to enter them, so I knew this was not a phobia or lack of confidence.

The fact is, he was confusing excitement for nervous low confidence, think about it, when we get excited we get butterflies in the stomach and the adrenalin pumps, this is the "Fight or Flight Responses" as explained earlier in this book, which caused him to vomit. This build-up of adrenalin, due to the excitement of the bike race, is almost the same emotion as nervous, low confidence of the "Fight or Flight Responses" which is acute stress, but in this case it was a good thing, as it gave him the energy boost to be aggressive in the races, it drove him forwards to succeed. The two emotions had been confused in the mind of the client; he was choosing to describe the emotion to himself as lack of confidence, when it was really the excitement over the build-up to the race. Once I explained the mind model to the client and the "Flight or Fight Response" (acute stress), and that he was confusing excitement with nervous low confidence, he agreed that I was right. The rest of the session was a standard confidence boost, as I will explain later.

This client never had a real problem; he just lacked understanding of his own mind with his reaction to the build-up to a race. This same lack of understanding from sports people is a regular occurrence. I have worked with many boxers; one that comes to mind was a young man who was a lightweight boxer. He wrongly thought that he could no longer enter the ring and so he wrongly assumed his career was over, due to the anxiety attacks he was having before a fight. He had been in a situation where he couldn't enter the boxing ring anymore due to feelings of vomiting and nervousness. Again this was a confused emotion and was really excitement, and an adrenaline rush from the "Fight or Flight Responses" and not nervousness at all. I explained this in detail with the client and once again he agreed the same as the dirt biker client had. His conscious mind wanted to continue boxing, but his subconscious had been playing a different movie of nervous tension, and as you know the subconscious always wins. Regardless I was very confident I would get him back in the boxing ring, so due to him being a boxer I changed my approach in this type of session because I didn't want him to lose the "Fight Response" and I didn't even want him to control it by stopping it. I wanted him to move that adrenaline rush (acute stress) from his body into his fists in order to build energy and power, so therefore confidence in the boxing ring to win his next fight. Therefore whilst the client was under hypnosis I used timeline and took him back within his mind to a time where he had what he wrongly thought was an anxiety attack. However, this time he had the knowledge that the emotion was the "Fight or Flight Responses" of an adrenaline rush of excitement. I built on that emotion and associated it to the anchor of him making a fist, so that all the built up of adrenaline was now in his fist, making him more powerful than he had ever been.

Dear student, do you see how I am capable of adapting ideas and using techniques differently to do what is best for the client? You will also be able to do this in time, once your experience and confidence in the therapy room grows.

I instructed this client to witness himself in the boxing ring with this new powerful fist, so I was using an emotion that he originally thought was negative, and I reassociated it to his fist (new anchor) for a positive result. So the next time in the boxing ring when he makes a first in his boxing glove, the anchor is reactivated to trigger the associated emotion. This client became extremely confident with the feeling of having an iron fist full of adrenaline waiting to be released to hit and win his opponent. Weeks later after the session, I received a phone call from this boxer, he was excited and laughing because he had won his first fight after seeing me. He then told me that after winning the fight, and whilst still in the boxing ring he was so pumped up with adrenaline and confidence that he pulled a mooney (dropping his pants showing his bum) and this action almost got him banned from boxing, but it just goes to show how successful one session can be.

Another sports example with another one of my real clients. This man was a huge, powerful man who was entered into the "World's Strongest Man Competition." Once again, the same as the other sport examples, he felt anxiety before the competition event. He told me that he was sat having breakfast one morning when the letter arrived from the "World's Strongest Man Competition" which was excepting him into the competition. On reading the letter he felt sick and needed to go to the toilet, his mouth went dry and he could no longer eat his breakfast. Once again this is the classic "Fight or Flight Response" and the client lacked understanding of this and his own mind. Educating this client on the mind model and "Fight or Flight Responses" is what I needed to do, and once again I reassociated that adrenaline into his arms and legs to make him more powerful, which also built confidence, and he overcame the misunderstanding of his emotional reaction to the letter. He in fact, became excited by the content of the letter and his emotion was not lack of confidence as he had previously wrongly thought.

This same lack of understand of the emotional response to the "Fight or Flight Responses" was also present in a professional golfer client of mine. He was affected so badly that he could no longer hit the ball. This once again is a very simple session to conduct, simply educate the client, build confidence, and allow the client to see the success of achieving the overall goal.

Moving away from sports. This client was dealing with a depressive anxiety reaction to a relationship break up. The male client was so upset after a two year relationship ended that he could no longer function in life, and his overall cognitive health was affected, and his ability to work was at an all time low. Even though the relationship had come to an end, his ex was not showing any interest in building the relationship back. She would still text him several times a day to keep an eye on him, and this was making it difficult for my client to move on with his life. He would reply to her text within seconds of receiving them, and when she needed him, he was there. Basically, she had him wrapped around her finger, and he always jumped when told, so she would take advantage of this and use him when needed. She wanted to make sure he was not with anyone else, in other words, she wanted to stay in control of her ex, to fall back on when she needed. Hence the text: "I need you here now," even though at the same time she wanted to see other people, so she was playing with his emotions by giving him false hope of getting back together in a relationship. He would replay the same movie through his mind several times a day about how things could have been different if he had done A, B, or C, whatever that may be.

It is not healthy, living in the past, reliving the same movie over and over again with the hope of a different outcome. We cannot change the past, but we can change our reaction to it, and that is where I can help. He would read her text over and over again throughout the day because it gave him a sense of connection to her; again this is not healthy especially once the relationship has ended. I advised him to only reply to her text an hour after receiving it. This would break down her hold on him, so she would realise that he no longer was her puppet. I told him it was best to remove all the texts from his phone, due to the repeated reading making him ill, and after he had deleted them in the session, he started to feel better as a result. Throughout the session my client kept saying things like: "I wish she was more honest," "I wish she wouldn't lie," "I wish she loved me back" etc. Without him realising it, what was the client indirectly telling me? He was telling me that he was imagining his perfect type of woman, the type that loves him and tells the truth and within his subconscious he had implanted this imaginary woman onto his ex. But that is not who she was, so he didn't love her, he loved the idea in his head that he projected onto her. Basically his emotional thoughts of the perfect woman he had associated to his ex, so every time he saw his real ex-girlfriend, he was seeing a false-truth of who he wanted her to be. But she wasn't that imagined version and so this created disappointment, depression and a feeling of loss within his mind. We can rationalise that she was not who he wanted her to be, but he couldn't previous to a session with me. So the disappointment and depressive anxiety he was feeling, he thought was because the relationship had ended and not how we see it, that of her not being who he wanted her to be, and him being upset of the loss of a person that never existed. So, unknowingly to him, he was not upset over the break-up with his ex, he was upset over the split with his perfect idea of a woman, that he had imagined and associated onto a real person. That being the perfect person he wanted her to be, but she was not. I made him see the real person that she was and while he was under hypnosis he started to realise that he was not missing out on a relationship with her at all, because she was wrong for him. The person he was really missing never existed. I spoke to this client weeks later, as I do with all of them, and he had taken my advice and only replied to texts an hour later, then two, and three hours later. He was no longer her puppet. So, as I had predicted and told him, his ex had started to chase him for a relationship, due to her loss of control over him. Anyway, it was too late for her, because he had realised that she was not the woman for him. Again only one session was needed.

This next client came for pain control, but remember that just because a client tells you what they want from a session, it is not necessarily what they need. In fact he needed educating on the mind and his situation, a confidence boost, and not pain reduction at all. I knew this because it was obvious that his illness was psychosomatic from the information he gave me, and I needed to prove this to him. If I had done a pain control session with him, then I would have been validating and reinforcing his negative thought pattern and his destructive thought pattern had to change. His dad had died some years ago after having a stroke and going blind in one eye, and as my client got older, to the similar age that his dad had passed away, it was playing on his mind a lot of how his dad had died. This thought process started to cause him anxiety and stress because of the fact he was reaching the same age that his dad had died at. He started to believe that he was going downhill the same way as his dad had, even though he was not physically ill.

In contrast, remember the female client that feared death, her mum had a stroke and went blind and later died the same as this man's dad had, so it is interesting to note the difference in the client's reactions to the same situation. The woman, after her mum's death, feared death, and this man believes he is ill, dying many years after his dad's death. Months before a session with me and years after his dad's death my client, whilst driving home from work, started to think about the upsetting times he drove to the hospital to visit his dying dad, and this thought and the fact he was driving his car, reactivated an old anchor that had previously remained dormant for years. This anchor required two simultaneous specific needs to be reactivated, hence the years of delay. Firstly he had to be in his car driving, and secondly he had to be thinking of the time from the past that he had visited his dying dad. Clearly this client has been suppressing his emotions for years and now the triggered emotional trauma was associated to driving his car and the thought of visit his dying dad in the past which was the anchor that caused him to hyperventilate, which caused him to believe he was having a heart attack, which caused him to panic. This reinforced his negative thoughts that he was ill, with his health going downhill and all that negative, fearful, overwhelming emotion was then reassociated to just being in his car, with driving now being the only specific need to reactivate the anchor, with the association of the panic attack as the emotional trigger response. This new anchor was so powerful, that every time after he got into a car the anchor was reactivated and he panicked, and this had happened over twenty times in his car, even though he had not had panic attacks anywhere else. Such is the power of an associated link within the subconscious.

So clearly he wasn't physically ill, this was only a negative state of mind when in a car and so he did not need pain control or medical help. If it had been a real illness, then he would have been ill anywhere, but he wasn't, it was only when in a car. This is the snowball effect. His dad's death caused the client stress and he suppressed the emotion for many years, and because he did not deal with the grieving process as he should have done, the stress years later then escalated to hyperventilating and panic attacks due to a reactivated anchor, and it got worse. Due to lack of understand of his situation and his own mind, my client wrongly believed he was physically ill. As a result, he wanted to try and understand the feelings he was suffering from, so he had been reading medical books trying to find a solution to his pain, even though unknown to him, his illness was in fact psychosomatic. Remember that repeated negative or positive focused thoughts result in long-term organic change over time, and eight weeks prior to the session with me, my client's friend told him he had neck pains, and due to my client reading medical books he knew that neck pains could mean the start of a brain hemorrhage, so my client started to have pains in his neck, the same as his friend had told him he had, which then convinced my client that he and his friend both had a brain tumour. This of course was all in his imagination with the snowball effect getting worse. Even the doctors told him that there was nothing wrong with him other than stress and tension. Remember that when a person does not deal with an initial cause of neurological pain, in this case the death of his dad and not physical pain, then all that built up emotional pain has to go somewhere once the anchor is reactivated, and in this case it manifested its self in the form of believing he had physical illnesses and panic attacks. The mind model of the four reference points and the seven mind rules once again fit this client perfectly, as they do with all clients regardless of their problem. Read them again whilst thinking about all that I have told you about this client.

The subconscious four reference points:

(A) The subconscious mind does not know the difference between what is real or imagined.
(B) The subconscious also does not know the difference between good habits, or bad habits. A habit is a habit through repetition regardless.
(C) The subconscious has no concept of time, past, present or future with regards to associated links.
(D) The subconscious also works via associated links, which are memories, cognitive thought (a persons perception of fact or fiction, real or fake, true or false-truth), and emotions (pain or pleasure), that are associated (connected), within the mind to an anchor. This can be any sound, touch, taste, smell, or seeing a certain person (or behaviour), colour, object or place.

The seven mind rules:

1) Ideas or thoughts result in physical immediate emotional reactions.
2) The subconscious mind delivers what we focus on.
3) Repeated negative or positive focused thoughts result in long-term organic change over time.
4) Imagination overpowers knowledge within in the mind.
5) Fixed thoughts can only be replaced by another via the subconscious.
6) Opposing ideas cannot be held at the same time.
7) Conscious effort alone, results in opposite subconscious success.

He became so fixed on the idea he had a brain tumour that he started to have chest pains and blurred vision because that is the symptoms that were written in the medical books. This shows how powerful the imagination is, and proves that his illness is psychosomatic, caused by the mind. Thankfully as a therapist treating him I can use this to my advantage, because he is clearly a highly suggestible person. I know this because his friend told him that he had neck pains and then my client believed that he also had neck pains, he acted upon the suggestion, then read a medical book and acted upon the information from the book also. The doctors told him, after some simple basic tests and I quote: "There is not a cat in hell's chance of you having a brain hemorrhage or tumour." But his psychosomatic illness was so bad the doctors were forced to put him on anti-depressive drugs. To calm him further, they did a full brain scan that showed no tumour, but even that information did not convince him that he was not ill, so I was his last hope. In fact, by the doctors doing what they did, it made the client's condition worse by reinforcing his negative belief with tests and tablets.

The cause of all his original pain was from his dad's death that he suppressed for years because he could not handle the pain. That pain reactivated and affected him years later, so ordinarily you would think to just go back to the event-cause, deal with the bereavement and the effects he was suffering from will all disappear. However that is not the case here because his original pain had over time escalated and developed in to another separate life of its own, due to the reassociation of emotions because he couldn't deal with the true reason for the emotional pain (his dad's death), which as a result, caused him to have a psychosomatic illness and he became a hypochondriac.

Therefore just dealing with the trauma of the death of his dad would at this stage not have changed the hypochondria problem. In order to deal with a problem, the client has first got to understand it in full and so I had to deal with his response to his loss and the hypochondria. I first told him that he was a hypochondriac, which is a person who constantly believes that they are ill or about to become ill. I educated him on the mind model with regards to his situation, and the associated link of having panic attacks when in his car from the upset of the loss of his dad. Plus I explained to him the original event-cause of his problem and once a client understands a problem they can start to relax more and deal with it rationally. This understanding later allows him to deal with the grieving process that he avoided for many years. I also did a "Large Weight and Balloon Suggestion Test" to prove thought patterns can, and do have organic change on the body, the same as his hypochondria does. However this client was so stubborn in believing his warped belief system of illness that I needed to do more. Even though educating this client helps him to come to terms with his loss and his response reaction, it does not change the hypochondria problem. By solving the hypochondria problem added to the education and he will be able to relax fully, which makes it easier for him to finally grieve. Most psychotherapists would comfort him to try and change his hypochondria problem, by creating a good feeling anchor. Regardless of the main stream way of doing things, I did the opposite with regards to his imagined illnesses, because I knew I had to.

You won't find another therapist with this approach, but I knew what was best for him, so this is what I did. Whist the client was in light trance, and remember I knew he was suggestible anyway so this was easy, I added neurological pain, in the form of guilt towards wasting a doctor's time and tax payer's money on his imagined illness, when some child with a real illness of cancer could have had all that time and money spent on them. This neurological pain of guilt leads the client to avoid wasting a doctor's time, and therefore prevents him from having his problem reinforced by a doctor via the pills and more unnecessary tests. Sometimes you have to be cruel to be kind. Whilst talking to him I periodically led the client to concentrate on his left arm, by randomly saying: "Your left arm looks tense" and then I would continue talking about wasting a doctor's time and talking through the brain scan he had and all the cost involved. Then again I mentioned his left arm saying: "Your left arm looks tense and painful" and then I continued talking whilst creating neurological pain of guilt of time wasting and again I mentioned his left arm saying: "Your left arm looks painful" and then I continued on another subject. The client started to rub his left arm and he made a facial expression that he was in physical pain, so I asked him: "Is your left arm hurting you?" He replied: "Yes." Even so, he had no clue as to why his left arm had started to hurt him, because his arm had not been hurting him before he came to see me.

Dear student, look at the words I have underlined. I was subconsciously feeding him hidden messages that he was not consciously aware of. I was leading him to abreact to an imagined pain, in order to prove to him all his illnesses are psychosomatic. I then explained to the client what I had done and he then became consciously aware that I had been mentioning his arm, implanting the suggestion of pain. He then understood, because I had proven to him that he was highly suggestible and his illnesses where psychosomatic, and he, in a revelation moment agreed with me. I could see the relief on his face and I then told him that his arm was fine, perfectly fine and again he agreed the pain had gone. This was a man suffering a psychological problem, so I used that pain against him to create a positive change. I had proven him wrong and because he also wrongly thought relaxation was something that was not possible for him, I hypnotised him to prove him wrong again. Also hypnosis helped me to create a good feeling anchor, to change the associated link to the anchor of the car to being positive, and again he was amazed. The session was very successful in every way, after the education, the pain I created in his arm to prove my point, and the hypnosis relaxation part of the session all resulted in an amazing life changing experience for the client. He left feeling like a new man, free from pain, even though I had not done the pain control session that he was expecting. Another fascinating example of a real client of mine, I am sure you will agree.

A female client thought she suffered from lack of confidence and low self-esteem. She was a very attractive woman, in fact she had been a stripper in the past, which required great confidence, so I knew this negativity that she was thinking about herself must have been a recent development; otherwise she would not have been a stripper in the past. This client when asked confirmed that her problem was recent. The negativity of feeling lack of confidence and low self-esteem must have been conditioned into her from another person verbally abusing her. Please note that even though the negativity about herself was recent, that did not mean that the abuse had started recently, because it could have been playing on her mind for many years, for her to finally crack under the pressure. The fact that she was so attractive made me first think that her abuser must be jealous of her beauty and therefore the abuser is not as attractive. I knew that her abuser must be someone close to her, because in order to change someone's thought processes, unless her abuser is a therapist, then they must be in regular contact with the victim, unless a one off traumatic event has happened. My first thought was that her husband could be the abuser or someone at her place of work, but I quickly eliminated the work, because when asked she told me she didn't work. So I was left thinking the husband must have become overweight and not as attractive as he used to be, because she confirmed that no traumatic event had happened. I then asked her was her husband overweight and not as good looking as he once was, and her reply was yes. This confirmed what I was thinking, that being within his mind he had to control her and so he lowered herself worth to make her think no one else would be interested in her. All this was due to his insecurities about himself due to him gaining weight and not feeling worthy of such an attractive woman that was his wife. So it was obvious that he was jealous of his wife's good looks and he saw other men as a threat to his relationship, as I am sure that many men would show interest in her by looking, and the fact that he knew she could leave him at any time for any man she wanted, hence the abuse to control her.

Dear student, do you see how by simply looking at this client's attractive appearance, and knowing her past job as a stripper, I knew without her first telling me, that this negativity was recent and she had not felt this way in the past. I also knew the abuser was someone close to her, because if they were not, then she would not be feeling this negativity about herself because it could not have been conditioned into her by someone that was not in regular contact with her. By asking her about the appearance of her husband, my thoughts were realised, so I also knew in all likelihood that the negativity she felt was brought on by his verbal abuse. He was jealous and feared losing her for another man. She showed no signs of physical abuse, so I ruled that out of the session, plus she had told me that there had been no traumatic event happen to her. I told the client that her husband verbally abuses her and puts her down all the time as a way of controlling her etc. Telling clients detailed information that they have unknowingly indirectly told me impresses them, some truly believe that I am reading their mind. This all adds to the belief in me, so this adds to the success that is achieved for the client. Of course I can work in this way because I am experienced so I can predict what has happened to a client due to working with so many clients and in time you will be able to do the same. Please note that predicting is not assuming, I never assume, I base my thoughts on the facts before me and experience, and it is the clients that assume things.

These are true examples of what her husband was doing: he took her in his car to pick up one of his mates and parked in a street waiting for the mate to arrive. My client saw the friend walking down the road, towards the car, in the distance and simply said to her husband: "Your mate is here now" his reply was, "Are you thick? Do you not think I have eyes? I can see him you know." That, of course was an unreasonable reaction to a simple comment from my client and events like that happened many times during the day. He would shout at her for simply forgetting to pull the plug out after having a bath, but yet when he forgot to pull the plug, my client told him and he shouted at her, "What are you telling me for? Just unplug it." Whatever she did, it was always wrong in his eyes. Even when he was in the wrong, he would take it out on her as all abusers do. It got so extreme, with him wanting to control her when he decided to spend tens of thousands of pounds buying his wife a hair salon business. My client had no training whatsoever in hairdressing, and she had never shown any sign of interest in it. So she told her husband that she was not interested in the business, even so he still bought it anyway. He expected her to make a success of it, which of course was a complete delusion, due to lack of training and my client having no interest in owning her own business. Of course, the inevitable happened, the business did not succeed. This gave the husband an excuse, once again, to put his wife down. He blamed her for losing thousands on the business, but yet beforehand she had told him it would not work. Regardless of the facts, he still within his mind, thought it was all her fault because she was useless and he told her that as if his version of reality was fact, it was only fact to him of course. My client told me: "Well, I've put up with it for twenty years so I might as well stay with him." There is no point in me telling the client how foolish her thoughts were because that causes confrontation, so, I said: "I have had a broken arm for twenty years; I might as well continue to put up with it." This made my client realise that she does not have to put up with it at all and it was time for change, she also realised that what she had said was not logical. I had ridiculed what the client had said, and not the client, which had a positive effect.

Dear student, do you see how I led the client to think differently? I did that without any disagreement of confrontation from me. It is not my job to advise a client to leave her husband, nevertheless, I can still make her see the situation for what it really is, then she can decide whether to leave him or not.

I helped her realise that she is in the right, and that it is her husband in the wrong, and she was simply a victim of his problem. An abuser can easily be identified by simple warning signs. The first sign is that abusers make alterations to the victim's environment, they intend to bring about a change in a victims psychological condition by changing his or her external circumstances. Hence why he bought her the business, it was another way to control her. The abuser is always defensive, and has a tendency to blame every mistake, failure, or mishap of theirs on others, or on the world at large. They never assume personal responsibility, never admit their faults or miscalculations and always blame the victim or others. For instance they say, "You provoked me," or "Look what you made me do." They are hypersensitive, picking fights by arguing unnecessarily. They treat animals, children and mostly the opposite sex impatiently or cruelly and they express negative and aggressive emotions towards the weak. They may have a history of violent behaviour coupled with vile bad language, threats, and hostility towards others. Sex with an abuser is almost like rape, because they want to control; they are forceful in and out of the sexual intercourse, they like physically hurting others, or find it amusing. They take control of the victim's destiny, for example, as this client's abuser did, bought her a business so she will abandon any plans she had, even though she was not interested in hairdressing. They do not respect people's boundaries or privacy, and ignore other people's wishes; they treat the victim as an object, or an instrument of gratification. The abuser always has to be in control of any situation and interrogates the victim if they have not seen them for a few hours. They make insulting jokes and remarks. Permission is needed if the victim wishes to go out, or do new things, even if it is simply meeting a friend or family members. They are patronising, condescending, and criticise people often. They are wildly unrealistic in their expectations from others, and life in general. In short, they have a low opinion of themselves and take it out on others. It makes them feel better when the victim feels worse than they do; it gives them a sense of pleasure feeling that someone else is weaker than they are. The truth of the matter is that these abusers are weak, pathetic individuals that need a sense of control over others; it gives them a sense of delusional power and it is the victim that is strong for seeking help. Once a client knows the facts of the situation, that being that they are the one in the right and it is the second party that is weak, they feel so much better about themselves.

The session continues, as explained in the script later. This client has since left her husband and I know this because I have seen her dating a handsome fit and healthy man that was treating her with respect, so he could not possibly have been her husband. She was in a club and she seemed very happy, and even though she did not acknowledge me with eye contact or words, she did notice me. Once she realised who I was she walked away from the man she was with and she came and danced in front of me smiling, and I am sure that was her way of thanking me by showing me that she was happy. After a few moments she walked back to the man she was with.

Anger Management Explained via Client Examples

Continuing with the topic of an abuser, but this time, the client was the abuser. The client was a young man in his twenties, who previously to a session with me, had been shouting at his girlfriend over a period of weeks, and this was causing them both great concerns. They truly loved one another but this shouting from the male was slowly breaking up the relationship. This was an anger management session with only the boyfriend present. My client claimed he knew the reason he was shouting at his girlfriend, however remember that as a psychotherapist you need to realise that a client's reality is warped and their perception of a situation is always wrong. He also told me that he did not understand why he could not control his anger towards his beloved girlfriend, or how to stop it.

Allow me to explain what was going on in detail. They had recently moved in together after four years of bliss in the relationship. They would travel together several weeks a year on holiday, and both loved each other's company on the holidays, days out and generally where ever they were, just by being together. The shouting from the male, my client, only started once they moved in together. My client would clean the house, make the evening meal and other household jobs before his girlfriend arrived home from work. He would even run a bath for her, and have all her clothes washed, ironed and a warmed towel waiting for her. He was a genuine nice guy, with highly respectable morals, and by seeking my help to save his relationship just showed that he was a nice caring guy, he just lacked understanding of his own new behaviour and he couldn't control the anger.

The start of his problem was in fact because he was so nice in doing so much for his girlfriend, and the reason being was that he wrongly assumed that his girlfriend would have the same moral beliefs, and do as much for him as he was doing for her, now that they lived together. There were times, when he was home from work later than his girlfriend, and therefore he expected her to have done the housework and prepared a meal, the same as he had done on previous days. Anyway, he would arrive home and she would be sitting in front of the TV with no meal ready, no bath prepared, with the clothes unwashed and not ironed. He would then shout at her for not doing the work, but at no point had he communicated with her beforehand what he would like done prior to his arrival home. Also, he had not considered what sort of day she'd had, so she could have had an extremely stressful day and just needed to relax. He was only considering himself, not the woman that he loved and he genuinely did not know this, because he was in his own version of reality and she was in hers, the two of them were not in a common reality with one another, due to lack of communication and understanding of one another's needs, behaviour and goals in their relationship.

This goes back to the mind model, my client, when travelling home from work, would imagine that his girlfriend will have done all the housework and prepared a meal for his arrival home. In his mind he had created a perfect world of everything being done, that he perceives as morally right. He would see, in his subconscious mind, his girlfriend waiting for him in a perfectly cleaned prepared home, and this imagined thought gave him a feeling of pleasure. So when what he had imagined was not the real situation on returning home, he would shout in disappointment by taking his frustration out on his girlfriend. Once again, whether it is real or imagined, it is the client's reality, so this must be explained to the client. He was in a different reality to that of his girlfriend. So, what he was shouting about was actually created in his own mind. He was unknowingly angry at realising that the real situation was not what he had previously imagined. He was his own worst enemy. The client told me that he had expected the same nice treatment that he gave her, but yet he had never told her that. Lack of communication with his girlfriend just added to the problem. He needed to tell her what he would like, but he had not, so the situation was my client's fault, not his girlfriends. Just because he decided to do nice things for his girlfriend without her asking, that does not mean she has to automatically do the same for him. He was blaming his girlfriend for him shouting at her, and all abusers blame the victim, even though it was his fault, the difference here to most abusers is that this client did not know he had become an abuser, and once I told him, that created guilt. Remember that the client had said that he knew the reason he was shouting, his perception was that he was shouting because he wasn't getting the same nice treatment that he was giving her, and therefore in his mind it was her fault, as if she deserved to be shouted at. Even though that was just his perception, the real reason that he was shouting was due to his imagination and his failures of communication. Therefore the situation was in fact his fault and not the girlfriends at all.

Now let us look at this same situation from his girlfriend's point of view. She is sitting at home, knowing her boyfriend will arrive home soon and I am sure she was looking forward to seeing him. When he enters the living room, the girlfriend is expecting a nice: "Hello" and maybe a kiss, but he starts to shout at her, and that creates a startled response in the girl's mind, because she was not expecting a raised, angry, abusive voice from the man she loves.

Dear student, do you see what had happened there? My client had unknowingly created an associated fear of him within his girlfriend's mind, because from that moment forward, the girlfriend will associate fear, from the startled response, to the arrival of her boyfriend getting home and shouting. You may be thinking that the boyfriend has created a phobia of himself within his girlfriend's mind from the started response; however this is not a phobia, because the fear is real and not irrational. Also the associated emotion of fear was rightly associated to the cause (the boyfriend) and the startled response cause was not from a separate, unrelated fear that had been wrongly reassociated to the boyfriend (anchor). Therefore this is not a phobia, it is a genuine fear reaction of the situation that is rightly within the girlfriend's mind associated to the boyfriend who created the fear. My client was pushing the woman he loves away, and once again, that was all explained to the client so that he understands and has an explanation of his own behaviour and what he is doing to his girlfriend. He had never considered the situation from her view point, but now that he understands more, I have compounded the feeling of guilt within him so that he avoids shouting at her in the future.

For my client to now know all this new information and now understand the true situation was a revelation for my client. It created a sense of guilt and embarrassment, within his mind, of what he had done, and that is the positive path towards change. At this point in the session the client now knows the real reason he was shouting, and he also knows why he could not control his anger towards his beloved girlfriend. It was because his imagination had taken over, so he had lost control in the form of a habit of shouting. Plus the fact that he did not understand the real reason why he was doing what he was doing, and the explanation for that is that he was shouting out of frustration of his imagined thoughts not being fulfilled, because it was not the same reality as his partner. All that information was explained as part of the mind model in relation to his situation. Regardless of the information I have already given him, he still does not yet know how to stop his bad behaviour, allow me to explain.

In the pre-talk section of the session I had led the client to feel guilt due to his behaviour and embarrassment of the fearful reaction he was having on his loved one. That led emotional state I then associated to the thought of his behaviour so that he will change by avoiding that aggressive behaviour after the session. The second part of the session was the hypnosis part, where I used aversion therapy in his timeline, to compound the associated neurological pain of guilt, and feeling ashamed etc toward his anger. This is what I did.

Whilst the client was under hypnosis, I took my client to a future event having never met me, whereupon returning home he found that his girlfriend had packed her bags and left him. This was devastating to the client and it provoked an abreaction in which I associated the emotion to the thought of his bad behaviour (anchor). Remember that the client must be aware that they have never met you, the therapist, and this future event will only happen if they continue the abusive behaviour. Then I made him realise that he has met me, and how lucky he is in the here and now, to have his girlfriend in his life and a chance to prevent that devastating possible future event. Then I ended the session on a positive, by reactivating an anchor with the association from a pleasurable emotion he had felt whilst travelling with his girlfriend. I did that by simply feeding back information he had given me in the pre-talk, so that he now realises what he has in life and this caused an amazing, positive change in his behaviour.

Dear student, because I have provoked and associated pain towards his negative, emotional outburst within his subconscious, is he ever going to shout at his girlfriend again? No, because he wants to avoid reactivating the anchor with the association of guilt and embarrassment and the fearful emotion I created of losing his relationship, which prevents him from getting angry and shouting at his girlfriend from there onwards. Also because I made him realise how lucky he is to have her in his life, so again he wants to avoid the negative anchor. If I had not used neurological pain towards his anger, would he have changed long-term? No, and that is why an abreaction towards a negative is so important for long-term success, never use the easy option of simply provoking pleasure to change as explained in the chapters: "Neuro Associative Conditioning (NAC) or Neuro-Linguistic Programming (NLP) and Abreactions", in the Volume One Book. Obviously all this had now stopped his bad behaviour.

I saw this client a few months later around town, and he looked at me, but no words were passed between us. As I walked passed him, we simply looked at one another and he gave me a large respectable smile, as if to say: "Thank you." On walking passed him I placed my hand on his shoulder, as if to say: "You are welcome," I then smiled, and I walked away.

Dear student, do you realise what I had done there? The emotion he was feeling towards me of gratitude and pleasure of saving his relationship, I reassociated to my hand on his shoulder within his subconscious, which became an anchor. Therefore at any point in the future should he ever need my help again for another reason, I can simply create good feeling by touching him on the shoulder to reactivate the anchor. The reason no words were spoken between us is because I knew he did not want his mates to know who I was, because his session was private and confidential, I didn't want to embarrass him. It was a nice moment between two men who both understood the situation, so no words needed to be passed between us. In that instance we were both in a common reality that was very different to everyone else in the room, so no other people would have known how powerful that moment was, only him and myself. What a wonderful skill to have, to be able to have such a positive influence over another human's life.

☐

Dear student, I am going to set you some tests from this real example of another client of mine. He came for anger management. I will explain his situation and then ask you some questions as the test. On a daily basis he was shouting at his two young daughters for trivial matters that did not justify his level of anger towards them. After he had told me he had two daughters, he continued and said:

"I love my children, but for some unknown reason I keep shouting at them over nothing, and I want to stop before I damage our relationships. If they are making a little noise as kids do, I shout, or if they have left a toy on the floor I scream at them, as if I'm totally out of control. This worries me because they are starting to fear me, I don't want to shout at them, but I can't help myself."

Dear student, with the limited information he has told me, I already had a very good idea of what the cause of his problem was. This is your first test. Can you read into what he has said and work out what his problem is with regards to the cause? I am not asking for details of the event-cause, just the basic cause. I will give you a clue. It is more important to realise what he has not mentioned, that is the likely cause of his problem. So my main question is: "Have you noticed what he has not mentioned that is the likely cause of his problem?" Take a moment to read again what he has said, and think about what he has not mentioned, that he should have mentioned, because what he has not said is the root cause of his problem. Also as a second test, I want you to read through what he has said, and understand his emotional state of what is going on in his mind. Spend five minutes on that before reading on, and please don't cheat because you are only cheating yourself. Think before you read on to get the answer and stop reading now!

I am going to go into detail with some of the things this client had said to me and I will explain the hidden meaning to his words. Firstly he said, "I love my children." So obviously I now know he loves his children, so they are not the real cause of his problem. He is therefore using them to vent his anger from the emotional pain that has been caused from another source. Remember that there is always a cause and an effect, the anger towards the kids is the effect and they are clearly not the cause of his neurological pain, plus the fact they are doing nothing wrong, they are just being kids. Of course the client could be lying to me when he told me he loves his children. Yet I know he wasn't, due to the emotion in his face that I observed. Plus he also re-confirmed to me that the cause of his anger is not the kids because he said: "For some unknown reason I keep shouting at them." When a client tells you that they do not know the cause (unknown reason) of their problem, that information is there conscious mind talking, because of course the subconscious does know the cause of the neurological pain, I just needed to find it.

As an experience psychotherapist what else do I now know as fact from those first sixteen words he spoke? "I love my children but for some unknown reason I keep shouting at them over nothing." With what he had said to me he had, unknowingly to him, indirectly told me that the memory of the cause of his anger is either a repressed (kettle effect) or suppressed (motivated forgetting) memory, due to the emotional hurt that a past traumatic event has caused him, which clearly continues to hurt him emotionally, so he is still feeling the pain from the event-cause, hence the effect of anger venting on his children, which has been caused from the traumatic event-cause. However I had a very strong thought that this was not a repressed memory; it was suppressed memory of the event-cause, which means he himself was trying to forget, but yet he couldn't, and I thought that because even though he said: "Unknown reason" of the cause, he had not mentioned something that he should have, and as a result I knew that he was consciously making an effort not to tell me the cause because it was too painful for him to except, even though he knew the cause. Hence the reason I knew this case was not a repressed memory, instead it was a motivated conscious effort to forget memory (suppressed memory).

Now do you know what he has not mentioned? Let's continue. He compounds his love for the children by telling me: "I want to stop before I damage our relationships." So I know my assessment of his true love for his children is correct, so again, they could not be the cause of his problem. What is more enlightening to me is what he had not mentioned. Have you worked out what the cause is? As your trainer I asked you: "Have you noticed what he has not mentioned, that is the likely cause of his problem?" Have you thought? This is so simple for me to work out, when he said: "I want to stop before I damage our relationships." He was referring to his daughters, but yet he never once mentioned his wife or girlfriend, or the children's mother and maybe the mother is his wife or girlfriend. It was a red flag to me that he had not mentioned the mother of the children when talking about not wanting to damage the relationships. So the explanation for his conscious effort of not mentioning her must have been due to the associated emotional pain he felt when thinking about her, and that pain he was trying to avoid, hence the suppressed memory, but the emotional pain had to go somewhere, so he was venting it out on his children. So the mother who he must have had a relationship with at some point, must no longer be around, because if she was still around, then the relationship with her would also be damaged because she wouldn't want him putting fear in to the children's lives. If she had still been around the family home, then he would have mentioned her, but he didn't. Plus when he talked about shouting and the fear the children were feeling, he again never mentioned the mother. So what about her feelings? Was he shouting at her also? I didn't need to ask, because it was obvious that she was no longer around the family home. My thought processes from this red flag realisation of no mention of the mother, was setting off alarm bells in my mind. His wife or girlfriend, the children's mother, must have either broken up the relationship with him or she had died, and that is why she is no longer around, which is the cause of his anger. To mention the mother would have been normal, but due to the fact he had not, meant he was suppressing a hurtful emotion from the thought of her loss, hence why he made a conscious effort not to mention her, and conscious effort means he was trying to suppress, so it was not a repressed caused memory. This is what made me think that her loss was either from breaking down the relationship, or she had died, which was the cause of this man's anger.

Dear student, do you see how I have received a lot of information from the simple first few sentences he had said to me? To do that is a skill in its self and the information gathered may seem obvious, now that I have brought it to your attention, but to most therapists it is not obvious. Had you thought that before I told you? If so, then well done. If not, then it's fine, because it will come with experience, and experience starts by reading and re-reading this book once finished, so that with the help of my teaching, you will remember these skills.

Once again do you see how I have received a lot of information? Not just by what he said to me, but from what he had not said. As a result of my insight, I felt very confident that I was right, but I needed to know for sure, so I said to the client in a sympathetic tone: "The children's mother is no longer around is she." Now what I said was not a question, it was me telling the client information that he thinks he has not told me, and granted he had not verbally; he had told me indirectly, by not mentioning her. Please note that what I said was open ended, because I did not say she had died, and I did not say she had ended the relationship. I implied that I knew she had either died or left the family home by ending the relationship, I was covering both avenues by my open ended use of words. I knew he hadn't ended the relationship because he was the one suffering from the event-cause. His reply to what I said was: "Yes she has died, but how did you know that?" Fact is I didn't know, but I didn't tell the client that, because his belief and trust in me is now concrete in my abilities. For the record this is how all psychics work and they do not have a paranormal gift, it is a skill, and I use the skill for good and they use it to con people out of money. I now have what seems to be a fifty percent chance of getting what I said next right. But the odds are higher in my favour because he was a young guy, so the likelihood is she died young, in an accident and not illness. So I said: "Was it an accident?" Once again my analysing of this client had proven to be correct, this is intuition or skill as a therapist that you either have or you do not. It emerged that she had died the year before in a car accident. Obviously this man was in a huge amount of emotional pain, and as previously mentioned, he was venting that pain (effect) out on his children from the bereavement event-cause, because he had never come to term with the loss, which makes it clear to a good therapist that he had not grieved due to being in suppressed denial of the loss of his partner.

Dear student, this is your next test. Would you use neurological pain towards this man's problem to provoke an abreaction? Or would you comfort him with pleasurable thoughts of the past and future with his children? Think about the question before reading on, but by now you know how I work, so you know I used neurological pain, but you don't know how in detail, even though you may be thinking, make him feel guilty. I can assure you that no counsellor or psychotherapist would use neurological pain with this type of client and that is why they fail long-term. By provoking pain towards shouting at the children and pleasure by not doing, means the problem is permanently solved, instead of a temporary fix with a doctor's pill or just by using on its own a good feeling anchor. Remember that this man is already in pain, so use it for the greater good, to save his relationship with his children and to help him move on with life. Also you would be saving the children from being emotionally damaged for life. This is what I did, but firstly, let me remind you to pause to build on the emotional pain. I said to the client the following in a commanding tone:

"Do you realise that not only have your children lost their mother, but they have also lost their father as well (slight pause) because you are not the man you once were, (slight pause.) You are hurting from the loss of your partner (slight pause) but your children are hurting more because they have lost both parents, (Slight pause.) You have been so wrapped up in your own grief that you have not once stopped to consider your children's feelings, (slight pause.) You love them (slight pause) but yet you have been so selfish towards them, (slight pause) taking your pain out on them (slight pause) by thinking only of your loss and not theirs. Am I (slight pause) right?"

That very powerful short speech from me had a dramatic effect on the client and he replied: "I had never looked at it that way, but you are so right" as he spoke those words he started to cry which is fantastic, because it was a release of a suppressed built up emotion that needed to be released, and this was clearly an abreaction.

Dear student, you felt emotional whilst reading that didn't you? Well don't, because as a good therapist you cannot allow emotions to affect you, you must keep in control of yourself for the benefit of the client. When I am working with a client that has an emotional story to tell, I myself show no emotion, because to me it is just a story and not real, even though it is real. I have the ability to close off and become the therapist, and after a session I become me again and I leave the therapist behind, so that my life and emotions are not affected in anyway by what a client tells me. Anyone that cannot control their emotions can never be a good therapist. Let us continue with this client. Do you see how he was in a warped reality? He had never seen his situation for what it really was, because he had not wanted to confront it, due to the hurtful nature associated to it. His mind had stopped functioning correctly due to stress and a sense of loss, as explained in the kettle analogy in the Volume One Book. To build even more neurological pain from the guilt of shouting at his children I added in a sympathetic tone:

"Your two little girls are too young to fully understand why their mother is no longer there and you have been adding to that confusion by shouting at them. How are they meant to understand? They have started to think they are bad people, even though they are being punished for a crime they are innocent of. They look-up to you as a role model, their daddy, so it is time to once again become the father you once were. The only thing your children ask of you is your love and care, and you do love them, so it is now time to move on with your life, for your sake and that of the children, because that is what their mother would want."

I used the words: "Would want" and not: "Does want" in order to allow his mind to realise that she is gone as in past tense, this helps with his grieving process. As regards pausing, I am sure by now you know where I paused. This was an extremely successful session and I know that as a student you are surprised with my approach, even so, I am also sure that you are in agreement with me that what I did for this client was in his, and the children's best interests. Obviously I left him on a positive high, of knowing how lucky he is to have two beautiful children in his life, and that helps him through his depressing time that he can now come to terms with and move on.

Start here, Boosting Confidence Pre-talk

What follows is the Pre-talk to the hypnotic induction. I have written both the pre-talk and what is said under hypnosis, far longer than it needs be. I have done this purposely, to give you more examples of what can be said and so that you can pick and choose what you may feel fits that particular client best. So, in short, this script is not intended to be read word for word to the client. It can even be used in a number of sessions if needed, to make them different from the previous, and please remember to always personalise a session to the client.

I always start by asking the client about their problem and situation to gain the information needed for the session. This time also allows me the time needed to build rapport. I then ask: "Do you agree that there are two parts of the human mind, the conscious mind (their conscious will) and the subconscious mind (their imagination)?" All would tend to agree with that there are two parts.

Please note, I never mention the third part of the mind, the analytical area of the mind to a client, because they do not need that information. So keep it simple. I only gave that information to you because you are my student, and of course, you are not training a student, they are a client, so the two parts of the mind is all they need to know.

I then ask the client: "Which part of the mind is in control of what you will be doing day-to-day?" And 99% of the time, clients will say: "The conscious mind." This is for two reasons: firstly, most people think they are consciously in control, and secondly, I also lead the client in the direction of saying: "Conscious Mind."

Dear student, how do I lead a client to say: "Conscious mind and why"? Think about that question, because the answer you have already been taught and therefore you know, even if you think you don't know.

This is what I do. I ask: "Do you agree that there are two parts of the mind, the conscious mind and the subconscious mind?" When I say: "Conscious mind," I lift my left hand, and by doing so I have created an anchor within the client's mind of the thought of: "Conscious Mind" being associated to my left hand, which is the anchor. I then put my left hand down and then when saying: "Subconscious Mind," I raise my right hand, and therefore by doing so I have created an anchor (right hand) associated to the words and thought of the: "Subconscious Mind" and then I put my right hand down. I then ask the client: "Which part of the mind is in control of what you will be doing day-to-day?" At the same time of asking that question, I reactivate the anchor with the association of thinking of the: "Conscious Mind" by simply raising my left hand, and so the client is led to answer the question by saying: "Conscious Mind" and then I put my left hand down. I then tell the client: "You are in fact wrong. It is the subconscious mind (reinforce the anchor by raising the right hand) that is in control and I will explain why later in the session" (then drop the right hand). I then reassure them that everyone gets it wrong and that avoids any confrontation and prevents the client from feeling foolish.

Dear student, can you think of why I have done that? Why had I led the client to think and say: "Conscious Mind" when it is wrong? How do I benefit from this as a therapist? Well I benefit in five ways as follows:

First benefit, I now know the client can be led, and therefore they are suggestible, which makes the session easy.

Second benefit, I also created a third anchor, can you work out what the third anchor is? It is not an obvious one, so I wouldn't expect even an experience therapist to figure out what I have done. I'll give you a hint. The first anchor was my left hand associated to thinking of and therefore saying the: "Conscious Mind." The second anchor was my right hand associated to the thought of the: "Subconscious Mind" and the third anchor was created once I said: "You are in fact wrong, it is the subconscious mind." It was at this point that the third anchor was created when I reinforced the second anchor by raising the right hand.

Even though I have given you that information, I still wouldn't expect you to have worked out what the third anchor is or what it is for, if you have, then well done you. When I lifted my right hand a second time I was reinforcing the second anchor to the thought of the subconscious mind. However because at that point I had made the client aware that the subconscious was the right answer, I had also then quickly changed the second anchor (right hand) to now thinking it's right (correct answer). So now the second anchor's association has been changed from thinking of the subconscious mind to realising it is right, it is the correct answer. Once the new association to the anchor (right hand) was created, I put my right hand down, so that the associated link to being right remained to be used again later in the session.

So I can class this as a new second anchor or third anchor with the original association to the second anchor having now been replaced. Remember the subconscious can only ever remember the last thing that was associated to an anchor. In this case the new thought of knowing it is right (correct answer) to the anchor of the right hand. The original association to the second anchor was: "Subconscious Mind" but that association had served its purpose and was no longer needed, so I replaced it for the added benefit of leading the client to associate the right hand to represent the right answer, the correct answer, which implies the right thing to do. I can use this anchor later in the session when I want to provoke, or lead the client to the right answer to whatever future question I ask them. Notice that I use the right hand for the right answer and not the left, hence why: "Conscious Mind" association was left hand, as it was the wrong answer. If I had made the right hand as the anchor for the wrong answer, then it would not have had the same use, and it would have been confusing for the client due to the word: "Right" hand being used for wrong and not right. Always use right hand anchor for a leading signal for the right answer or right thing to do, as in my opinion it should be. I will be using this signal anchor later in the script.

Third benefit of leading the client to say: "Conscious Mind" is the creation of a "Trans-Derivational Search (TDS)" within their mind by me replying with saying: "You are in fact wrong, it is the subconscious mind that is in control and I will explain why later in the session." By saying that I created a: "Trans-Derivational Search (TDS)" within the client's mind because they are now consciously wondering how could they be wrong. How can it be the subconscious that is in control, and I wonder how he is going to explain this? This sent the conscious mind on a journey and therefore bypassed via TDS, which opens up their subconscious to suggestion, which cements the anchor of right hand meaning right answer, the right thing to do.

Fourth benefit is that the client's subconscious knows I am in control. When a client is led to answer wrongly, they accept that they were wrong because I proved to them, with my knowledge that I am right. The client knows that I am right, and so they will agree to all future suggestions and commands from me as being right. I have become the authority figure of reason, truth and knowing what is right. My knowledge gains the clients trust in me. This way I avoid confrontation within the session because the client knows I must be right throughout, regardless of any opposing ideas they may have previously had.

Fifth benefit is that the client is now in light trance due to the TDS and rapport built.

I continue by asking for information about the client, that way I can personalise the session to suit them. I ask what have they tried in the past, and what their routine is at the moment. I personalise the pre-talk based on the information the client provides from my questions. I ask other questions and say things like:

1) What methods have you tried to overcome your problem?
2) Have you had any success with any of those?
3) What's the most important reason for you to overcome this problem?
4) What are your ambitions in life?
5) What have you achieved in life? For example in your job, family or home etc.
6) What are your strengths?
7) Tell me about a happy time in your life when you felt confident and relaxed, if you can't think of one from the past, then tell me about a future event that would make you happy, feel good, warm and comfortable, in a quiet place.
8) Tell me about a situation and the events that led you to feel low confidence, nervous or depressed, run me through the scene from start to finish.
9) Tell me, is there a song or a tune that makes you laugh? It could be from your childhood like the Muppet Show, something like that. If not a song, then a situation or person, a character from a movie may be.
10) What do you think is the event-cause of your problem?

Dear student, the information gathered from the above questions can be used later in the session. The more information I have on their problem, the more successful the session will be, because it becomes a more personal experience of a session to them. I always tell my clients: "Personalised sessions are far more successful than group sessions. That is why I do not do group sessions because each individual is different and you are the only person that matters at the moment." (By saying that, it makes the client feel important.)

Below I have written some of the reasons why your client may have low confidence and how they can change through hypnosis. They will be able to relate to some, if not all of the points below. If so, then they are a perfect client for a confidence boost session with you.

I've always lacked confidence, even when I was a little

Confidence is learned, not inherited. So if you lack confidence, it probably means that you were criticised or undermined as a child. Relax, because that lack of confidence is not permanent; you can still change.

Think back. What negative early messages were you given? "You are useless. You can't do things." Then take each message and contradict it. If your message was: "You are not popular," remind yourself of the friends you have and stick a message on your mirror, "People like me." Which is an affirmation. Act as if you are popular and you become popular. You can rethink the past. You can reinvent yourself, and hypnosis will give you the boost that you need, because remember, you need to make a change subconsciously before it can be conscious. (Explain the mind model to all clients).

I see myself falling flat on my face and then I do

What you think, will happen, so if you think you're a failure, you'll fail. Confident people think themselves successful and they find success, even though their confidence most of the time was an act. They literally run a kind of internal "Home Movie" where they are doing well. If you find yourself in a situation that you once felt nervous, then to prevent that nerve-wracking feeling, you can run through a positive internal "Home Movie" of yourself in a situation, before you are really in that same setting. If you're going for a job interview, imagine just how well you'll do and tell yourself you're going to succeed. Even if you don't get the job, you'll naturally do better than if you had imagined the worst.

I typically feel so nervous inside, that I sabotage myself

When we get stage fright, butterflies are useful by reminding us to give our best performance, but if we allow the "Fright, Fight or Flight Response" to take control, that can make us so physically nervous that we fail. The answer is simple: by faking it you can often end up feeling confident quite naturally. This is what people do that look confident. So just before that important piece of work or that big date, you need to relax, then stand tall, hold your head up, relax your shoulders and stand with your weight evenly balanced over each foot. Smile to raise your spirits. If your mouth is dry, bite your tongue to release saliva. Take a deep breath and go for it. Play a positive movie in your mind of being in control of yourself and looking confident.

Regardless of how good I feel, I often look nervous to other people

If you act as though you lack confidence, other people will react to that, and often badly.

Use the "SET" plan – Smile, Eye contact, Touch, which picks up on the three elements confident people typically demonstrate:

1) Smile and you will look relaxed.
2) Hold eye contact and you will look sure of yourself.
3) Touch with a firm handshake or even just a pat on the arm and you will look in control.

I sometimes feel unsure when I am doing something new

This statement sounds negative. Isn't it bad to feel unsure? Actually, this is in fact, a positive strategy in some new circumstances, because it's no good feeling falsely sure in all new things, because you could be too confident and not see a potential danger. With something new, feeling unconfident is your mind's way of alerting you to your lack of experience or a potential danger.

So this is a positive thought pattern, but you may have wrongly seen it as negative, so your reaction to the new situation was wrong. You need to re-educate your mind to a new way of thinking and hypnosis will help you with this by gaining the relevant experience on a subconscious level. So with anything new, like that speech, those interview questions, that new skill, you simply practice ahead of time via your subconscious imagination.

Rehearsal will raise your performance, and in turn raise your confidence. You can, with hypnosis, rehearse different situations as if they are real within your own subconscious mind, because by doing so, speeds up the learning process in becoming confident at any given situation or task.

I worry that other people will laugh or disapprove of me

The secret here is that almost everyone feels like you do, which means that while you're busy wondering what other people think of you, they're busy wondering what you think of them. Work with that and help other people feel better, approach them, be friendly, ask questions, and compliment them. Then, not only will they like you, you will also be too busy concentrating on them, to be thinking about yourself.

I am confident in some areas, but I feel unsure in others

If there's one thing you can do with confidence, it's being able to transfer it across to: "Nervous" areas. Again, I will show you how with hypnosis, by associating good feeling to a previous nervous situation, that situation then becomes pleasant and positive.

If something feels too big for me, I just collapse under the pressure

What's the best way to eat an elephant? Answer is one bite at a time.

The moral here is that it is usually easier to do things in small chunks rather than trying all at once. So, break a project down into smaller goals. Or try a: "Practice run" and then build up from there. There is an exception to this: "One bite at a time" approach, because sometimes by doing the outrageously risky, you can boost your confidence because it makes everything else seem easy.

When I was a child I badly burned my leg in a fire, and as a result I feared fire and I would avoid it for many years after the accident. Anyhow I didn't want to go through life having an exaggerated fear of fire more than I needed to in order to avoid the danger, so I decided to do the outrageously risky option to confront my fear. I went and learned how to fire breath, and within the day I was putting flames out with my mouth, breathing fire and rubbing flames up and down my arms. It worked, I now feel very comfortable around fire. I also feared heights, so I went sky diving and the result was positive.

Confidence Mind Model

Dear student, this mind model sub-chapter can be adapted, and used for clients with low confidence problems, anxiety, depression, stress, jealousy, and even anger management. The following is said to the client:

The mind is split up into two parts. You have the conscious and the subconscious parts of the mind. At the beginning of this session you thought that you were consciously in control of your life, however as we continue you will realise that the conscious is the part of the mind that we would like to think is in control, but it is not, it is the subconscious mind that is in control.

For example: you do not think about breathing, blood circulation, making your heart beat, because the subconscious is the autopilot for the body, it is running the body twenty four hours a day, seven days a week. The subconscious part of the mind can do many things at a time and whilst it is running the body, it is also taking in two million pieces of information every second, passing on what it thinks is important to the conscious mind and disregarding the rest. For example: you buy a new car and you are driving down the road in your new car, now it seems like every other car is the same as yours, and they are even the same colour. Even though you cannot remember seeing so many of these same cars the day before. So did everyone go and buy the identical type of new car at the same time as you? No, of course not. The day before, the subconscious still noticed all these cars, but it thought that type of car was not important to you, so the subconscious did not pass the information on to the conscious mind. Therefore you were not fully aware of them even though they were there. But now you have got this new car, it has got to be important to you, because you first imagined buying and driving the car and then consciously did what you first subconsciously imagined. Because in order to do anything in life, we have first got to imagine doing it. So because you imagined it and then did it, the subconscious realises this type of car is now important to you, and so now it passes the information on every time it sees this type of car, so you are now consciously aware of seeing more of those cars than you have ever seen in your life.

You see, the two parts of the mind have become friends where the thought of this car is concerned. That is what you have not done with your low confidence problem, you have never imagined seeing yourself overcome this past problem, so there is still conflict with the conscious and subconscious mind, and when the will and imagination are in conflict, the imagination always wins, due to the subconscious being the more powerful.

You see, you have made a conscious decision to overcome the low confidence problem, but you have not been able to, because you tried to solve your problem on a conscious level, but your problem is within your subconscious mind and not your conscious one. Let me explain.

The conscious part of the mind is very logical and very rational. It is the part that you use when making your decisions on a day to day basis. But it is the imagination (subconscious) that determines whether we carry out those conscious decisions or not. Last week you may have made the conscious decision to go swimming, but then you imagined that the water was cold. How do you know? Because you did not go swimming, that imagined thought stopped you doing something, you had made a conscious decision to do. Therefore your subconscious mind is in control. This is what has happened with your anxiety, low confidence problem. You consciously want to overcome anxiety etc but you are still playing a different movie in your subconscious imagination. Again conflict is at work, so you will never win when only trying to overcome a problem consciously. The conscious is the part where your willpower is held, but of course, you have got to remember to use it. I know you can use it because you had the will to get up this morning, wash and clothe yourself, and you have had the will power to come here for therapy. So we know it is there.

The conscious part of your mind can think of only one thought or idea at once. This is why we can only concentrate on doing one task at a time when doing it consciously. However, we can do many tasks, but only one is conscious, and the others are subconscious, in the form of a habit, whether they are good or bad habits. The conscious mind is a very slow part of the mind. And this is why we get stressed out. We try to do too many things at the same time consciously and that part of the mind cannot do it. You know what happens: the phone rings, someone wants your attention and you are trying to cook the evening meal, you are stressed out because you try to do all three things at once. Take a step back, realise what is happening and do one task at a time. Doing one task does not get us stressed. Trying to do two tasks consciously starts the stress ball rolling. It is like a snowball rolling down a hill, the more tasks you try to do at once, the more the stress builds up, and once we get stressed out, we are now not able to do any of the tasks we were trying to do. Stop, take a step back in your mind and realise what is happening and why you are stressed and simply do one task at a time. That way you have a better chance of carrying out the entire task.

This stress build up makes your phobic or low confidence response even worse once confronted by the same situation, the anchor that triggers off the associated emotion to fear where you had a phobic response or low confidence previously. Then, over time, several phobic or low confidence feelings later, the subconscious part of the mind thinks: "I can do that job for you" and it took your problem on as a habit to free up your conscious mind's burden, so the subconscious thinks it is doing you a favour. Because all a habit is, is something you do consciously a number of times and then the subconscious will take it on as a habit. So trying to change it consciously is impossible, because the problem is now subconscious.

The subconscious part of the mind knows that you can only consciously concentrate on doing one task at a time, so the more jobs the subconscious can do on your behalf the better. As far as the subconscious is concerned, it is doing you a favour by taking on the problem as a habit, because also, the subconscious does not know it is a problem, it is just a habit that you want to do as far as your subconscious is concerned. It will keep the habit until you subconsciously remove the habit, by changing the negative associated link to a positive one, so that you feel comfortable about what was once unnecessarily fearful. And we will do that via hypnosis later. Driving is another habit. Again, when you first started to learn to drive you drove consciously, you had to think about mirror, signal, brakes, clutch, and what is going on around you. It was impossible to have a conversation because your conscious mind was occupied on the one task of driving, and that part of the mind can only do one task at once. But you passed your test and practiced and now you do not even have to consciously think about driving, because your subconscious has taken the task on as a habit, in order to free up your conscious minds burden. Now when driving down the road if someone pulls out in front of you, you just stop automatically, because you do not have to consciously think about driving. When you drive home from work, before you know it you are home and cannot consciously remember the details of most of the journey you have just had. You know the journey you have taken, because you take the same journey every day, so your subconscious has taken on driving that route as a habit, and so you subconsciously drove home, hence why you cannot consciously remember the full journey. That is called: "Highway Hypnosis." So hypnosis comes naturally to you. Your life is full of habits, for example: swimming is a habit, riding a bike, reading, walking, the way you brush your teeth, because you no longer need to give those tasks any conscious thought.

Our lives are full of habits, because a habit is only something you do consciously a number of times, which is then taken on by the subconscious as a habit, regardless of whether the habit is good for you or not.

Now, at the moment, the subconscious is protecting these habits. It does not want you to forget to drive as you drive down the road. It does not want you to forget to swim whilst swimming across a river. It is also protecting the habit of your anxiety or low confidence, because the subconscious does not know the difference between a good or bad habit. A habit is a habit through repetition as far as the subconscious is concerned. So it is still running the old emotions with the same reaction response of anxiety in the form of a habit. It is still running the same old movie of something it thinks you want to do and how it thinks you want to emotionally feel, so you are fighting between the two parts of your mind, because you want to consciously change, but you haven't told your subconscious that. There is the problem.

Your conscious knows all the reasons why you want to overcome your problem, but the subconscious is still rerunning the old reasons of associated fear of why you started the problem in the first place.

The subconscious holds all your memories and emotions. You have got memories stored within your subconscious going all the way back to childhood, but you cannot consciously always recall them. Then a song might come on the radio and all of a sudden you can remember a memory that you have associated to that song, who you were with, what you were doing, even what you were wearing in that past time, and you feel the emotions that you previously associated to that song. This is an associated link. When we experience two things together for a little while, one will automatically remind us of the other in the future. In the subconscious are your emotions and emotions are controlled by the subconscious, so due to the habit, you feel anxiety, low confidence, once that negative associated emotion has been triggered via the reactivated anchor.

Another reason you have not been able to overcome your past problem is due to lack of understanding of it and lack of understanding of your own mind and the responses you have been suffering from. Also your imagination is in the subconscious, and the imagination is very powerful. For example: you have probably had dreams or nightmares before and you have woken up shaking, sweating and your heart pounding, but yet you have not been anywhere, you are still in bed. Well this is because the subconscious part of the mind does not know the difference between something real or imagined, both are your reality. So if you are having a dream of running down the road scared, as far as the subconscious is concerned it is actually happening, therefore it makes physical, organic changes to the body, hence you wake up shaking, sweating and your heart pounding.

The problem is that a lot of the time when you try to overcome a fear you are consciously saying to yourself: "I am not nervous" (or whatever it may be). Well what are you imagining when you say that? Yes that is right, you are imagining and saying to yourself: "I am Nervous," so you are getting the subconscious to imagine fear, being embarrassed etc. That makes it challenging for you to overcome the nerves because the subconscious knows it has always associated certain situation, be them real or imagined, to feeling negative. So when you imagine a negative situation, you have implanted a powerful suggestion that sets of an alarm in your head to remind you to feel the fear, nerves whatever it maybe. The subconscious is reminding you to do something that it thinks you still want to do, and that is to feel negative (or whatever their problem is).

Remember that the subconscious mind does not know the difference between what is real or imagined, so just by imagining yourself being nervous, you feel real fear. Imagination (subconscious) always overpowers knowledge within your conscious, so you consciously want to overcome the problem, but your imagination within your subconscious is still playing the same negative movie in the form of a habit, that the subconscious does not know is causing you emotional harm.

Now what you have got to do is imagine it is going to be easy for you to overcome your past problem, and make it humorous. You have got associated connections with certain activities. For example: going on holiday to a hot country and feeling negative about yourself. You need to imagine those situations in a humorous way, and that is what we need to do today on a subconscious level, because that is where the problem is.

So the next time you are in the same situation, the subconscious just makes it easy for you. This is because you have already imagined what is going to happen when you are there, and so the subconscious will just make it easy for you because you have associated the situation in a humorous way. A new, improved associated emotion, instead of fear. The subconscious mind can only associate one emotion to an anchor, so we are going to change it from the neurological pain of fear, to pleasure. You see you have been telling yourself on a conscious level that you want to overcome your problem, but you have not been able to, because fear is associated within your subconscious mind to the situation (or whatever the client's problem is). It has become a negative habit and therefore positivity has not been passed on to your subconscious mind to override the fear, nervousness etc. You are consciously aware of negativity, due to still playing the negative movie within the subconscious.

So you have not been able to overcome the problem, because when the conscious will and subconscious imagination are in conflict, the imagination will always win, because it is the more powerful part of the mind. You have been going about it all wrong on a conscious level and this is where I come in, to help you on a subconscious level, through hypnosis.

So that is what you do in a session with me, you use the imagination under hypnosis to overcome the problem. For example: if you consciously think, do not think of a black cat, you have then imagined a black cat, making it impossible to stop imagining the cat. What you consciously wanted to achieve: "Do not think of a black cat" has had the opposite effect on the subconscious mind, and so you focus on the cat instead of something else to overcome the thought of the black cat. You have gone about your problem consciously and it has had the opposite effect. So again this is where hypnosis comes in, there is no magic trick or waving of a magic wand with hypnosis. It is a way of getting you to relax, and because you are relaxed I can talk directly to your subconscious, the part that is in control. Because I am talking to the subconscious, together we can rerecord an up-to-date movie, so that your past irrational problem becomes humorous and it is something you now feel comfortable about. I am only helping you to do something in which you already want to do, but in the past you have not known how. So we are taking away the old associated emotions to the bad habit, and replacing it with the new emotion of feeling good in that situation that you once felt bad. After the session you will feel great because you have both parts of the mind working as one, to keep you from feeling how you felt in the past.

As I have mentioned, the primary function of the subconscious is to protect habits, and by doing so it thinks it is protecting you. We know this because if pulled under the water when swimming, you automatically go to the surface and subconsciously swim, due to the protected habit of swimming in order to protect you from the danger of drowning. Your subconscious has also done the same with your problem, it has protected the habit because it thinks it is doing you a favour, just the same as protecting the habit of swimming. This is because your subconscious doesn't know the difference between a good or bad habit, and so the subconscious protects the habit regardless of the type of habit, even if it is harming you cognitively because it does not know that it is. You never told the subconscious, you only told the conscious, and the subconscious won the battle. So with my help using hypnosis, we will now replace and therefore remove the past associated emotions of fear and the old movie that was a conditioned habit of feeling nervous as you no longer need it. Then your subconscious will keep you free from those negative thoughts again, as you take on a new, positive associated emotion of thinking, or seeing spiders, or where ever you felt low confidence. So with hypnosis we are going to replace the old habit with a new positive move and emotion. We are going to get you to use the imagination to imagine it is easy, and then it will be, because it is, and by doing so we are going to remind the subconscious that it has got to protect the new, healthy ways of thinking and the positive new habit.

Dear student, basically explain the mind model to the client and cover the four reference points of the mind, and the seven mind rules were appropriate to their problem. There is one more thing to add to your script, with regards to the mind model. That is, the subconscious mind has no concept of time, so it will be easy to overcome the client's problem. You could say to your client:

"You see the human mind works by association. When we experience two things together for a little while, one (the anchor), will automatically remind us of the other (associated memory and emotions), in the future. That is also proof that the subconscious mind has no concept of time. Remember the subconscious mind reference point (C): "The subconscious mind has no concept of time, past, present or future." The associated links of memory and emotions to the anchor, will be the same age twenty years from now, the same age from the day you created the anchor, so you will still remember the event and (or just), feel those same emotions that you have associated to the song, as if you were back in that time, the day you created the anchor. This is due to the subconscious mind not realising that twenty years have gone by, it is as if it were yesterday. Your physical body has aged, but those associated links to the anchor, are the same age as the day they were created, and therefore the subconscious mind has no concept of time. This means that memories and emotions within the subconscious do not age, and also a memory and emotion are two separate things from the same event, hence why a memory can be repressed and the emotion be remembered. Why the memory can be repressed was explained in my Beginners to Advanced Volume One Book. Of course you consciously know past, present and future, but that is not where the associated links to the anchor are stored. A memory, emotion (associated links to an anchor), are stored within the subconscious. Even though a memory and emotion cannot be changed and are the same age throughout life, we can still create a new memory and emotion of the same event to the same anchor, in order to replace the old, via the subconscious, using hypnosis. This way we rationalise an event through an adult's perspective, instead of the child's old perspective, so that any negative effect that the associations to an anchor were causing, can be removed and replaced for new positive associations.

Dear student. In this script I am simply showing another way of explaining the information to make it more personal to the client's problem. Reading this script of ideas, you will realise that what the client is told, and what I have taught you to do as a therapist, the skills, the understanding of the client's problem and the way they think, and how I advise of how you need to think, are two very different mindsets. The therapist is using skills that the client is not consciously aware of, tone of voice, observation, building rapport, leading, etc. They do not know techniques like free association or the fact that you are bypassing their conscious mind via a TDS; they don't need to know your skills. As long as the client understands what you are saying, they don't need to know the real reason you say certain things, or your body language like the manipulation anchor at the beginning of this script to get the client to say: "Conscious Mind." That skill used both verbal and non-verbal manipulation that the client is not aware of consciously. All they need to know is the understanding of their problem, how to solve the problem and understanding their own mind. What the therapist is doing in the back ground is a skill the client will never be fully conscious of. You the therapist are in fact controlling two minds very differently, yours and the clients and yours will be always one step ahead of the clients, because you have the psychotherapy skill knowledge that they don't. So there is no need to fully explain what you are in fact doing to the client, just make sure that what you are doing works.

What Do You Know About Hypnosis?

Dear student, only say the following if the client is worried about being hypnotised, because the more they understand, the more they will relax around the idea of being hypnotised, because their negative worrying preconceptions are wrong. Continue:

Well, I cannot make you do anything that you do not want to do. This surprises some people because they see those hypnosis shows on the TV and it does make it look like they are making people do what they do not want to. Think about it, why do people go to see those shows? They go to be entertained, to see people act stupid. So then, they ask for a volunteer. Now who is going to volunteer? So the hypnotist entertainer has all these people on stage and he starts deciding who will be the most entertaining, who is the biggest show off. The people in the audience might be thinking that he is looking for people that are hypnotisable, but he is not, because he knows that anyone is hypnotisable, so he is looking for the biggest show offs, the ones that want to be the centre of attention, the biggest exhibitionists. Now he has got it made, he is not making them do something they do not want to do; he is making them do what they already want to do. And that is great because that is exactly what we are doing today. I am not making you overcome your past problem; I am helping you do something you already want to do. Hypnosis is a great way for getting you to do what you already want to do but couldn't, due to trying consciously. When you relax via hypnosis you will not fall asleep, you will be aware of everything. You hear the sounds outside the room, the sounds from in the room, you remember everything. You still have thoughts running through your mind, one of those thoughts might be: "Am I hypnotised?" Well the answer to that is yes, because hypnosis is a feeling of being relaxed, and because you are relaxed, I can talk directly to the subconscious part of your mind in order to help you overcome the past problem.

The best way to describe hypnosis is to say that it feels like first thing in the morning, you have just woken up but you have not opened your eyes yet, you know you can open your eyes if you want to, but you do not want to because you are so relaxed. You are going in and out of hypnosis all day long, without even realising it. The most common form of hypnosis is driving. You are driving down the road on a trip you have done a hundred times before and you start to daydream or think about something else. Next thing you know you get to your destination and you have no idea how you got there. That is: "Highway Hypnosis." Whilst driving, your conscious mind has wandered off and your more powerful subconscious has driven you safely to your destination, due to the habit of driving the same route many times in the past. Also, reading a book or watching the TV. You are at home and you are watching TV and you are hanging on every word that is happening. Someone asks you a question and you do not hear them, or you do not want to hear them, because you are so relaxed and don't want to be disturbed.

Now there are a number of ways to respond to hypnotic suggestions. For example: you could respond within your mind by thinking: "Yes" or "No." So if I make a suggestion of: "You are now ready to overcome the past problem" and you think: "Yes I am" then that suggestion will work, and it will work every time in working towards a positive result of achieving your goal. Another way to respond is to be uncomfortable with the suggestion. For example: if I say: "You are now ready to confront your fear" and you think: "No I am not" then that suggestion I made will be rejected, so you are in control at all times. I sometimes have people in therapy who have been sent to me by their husbands, wives, or doctors, and they say: "Get in there and sort your problem out" and like I said, I cannot make someone do what they do not want to do. So again the suggestion is rejected because that type of client is unmotivated, they do not want to overcome their problem. Another way to respond is to hope. Now, there is a problem with the word hope, it is the twin sister of the word try. If I try to pick up this pen up, I do not do it because I am just trying, if I want to pick it up I will. The subconscious is too busy doing a hundred and one other things to care if you are just trying. Therefore if you are uncomfortable, unmotivated or just hoping and trying then the subconscious has not got time to listen and so will just reject any suggestions. However by being motivated and wanting change for the better, and by you agreeing and liking the suggestions I give, and by you wanting this session to work, not only will the positive suggestions be accepted, they will also be acted upon.

Hypnosis is like a contract between two people. My part of the contract is to give you all the thoughts and therapies that I know are going to make you happier. Your part of the contract is to follow along with the suggestions, want them to work and allow them to work. Now I know I am going to keep up with my part of the contract. Are you going to keep up to yours? Good, then we are going to be successful.

Dear student, at this point you can do a suggestion test on the client as explained in the Volume One Book. This will prove to them how powerful the subconscious mind is, it also adds to the belief in what you have told them about the mind model. Have you noticed that the information just given in this sub-chapter contradicts what I have taught you? With regards to what is said to the client when talking about hypnosis, I wrote: "Well, I cannot make you do anything that you do not want to do." As a student you know that is nonsense, because under hypnosis or light trace we can instruct a person to do anything. Even though that is true, the client doesn't need to know that, because they would feel uncomfortable around you, so what was said was simply giving them a deluded sense of control, when in fact they are not. It made them feel comfortable around hypnosis and therefore the session can continue.

Then I continue after the suggestibility test by saying: "Do you have any questions before you start living the life you want?"

Induce Hypnotic Trance

Dear student, remember when inducing trance within your client, you must pause when appropriate, in order to allow the client's mind to process what you are saying, and this also allows them time to respond. I am not going to write when to pause in this induction script because every induction is different, due to being personalised to the client. The feedback loop effect from observation is also important, monotone of voice and don't rush, simply talk slowly, in a relaxed manor, mirror their breathing at times, and personalise the trance from information from the pre-talk, all of which I have covered in detail in the Volume One Book. Continue:

As we begin you will take note of the different sounds in the room, the sound of my voice and thoughts or images that may drift through your mind and that is fine. It is now time to relax, please stare at the ceiling or light, take in a deep breath and relax as we release this breath. Continue breathing deeply and exhale slowly as you are learning to relax. As we continue here today, feeling peaceful, both you and I want to remain comfortable as you listen and concentrate on what I am saying, because what I say is important to you in achieving relaxation here today and your goal. Simply let go of all the tensions now and enjoy the feeling of being relaxed. Now you must remember, as we continue to breathe in deeply and exhale, that sometimes you can hear my voice, as you can now, and sometimes it may seem very quiet, and at times it does not matter if you cannot consciously hear my voice at all, because you cannot turn your ears off and therefore your subconscious mind will still be taking in everything that I say. You cannot turn your sense of taste, touch or smell off and you cannot turn your eyes off, you will simply closed your eyelids over them, because you cannot turn your senses off, you are always in control. Take in a deep long breath, and hold it, then in a moment breathe out, and as you do so, you are releasing all the tension from the past day, week, month and year, that you may have experienced. Now allow your head to stay where it is and start to look down, as if you are looking down at your feet, even if you cannot see them. In a moment I am going to turn on some relaxing music that is going to help you relax even more as we continue.

(Turn backing induction music on)

Allow any thoughts you may have to float into the distance, as you become more and more relaxed as time goes by. Your eyes are now becoming so tired that they simply close, and as they do, you feel even more relaxed. Allow yourself to go to (yawn so that the client can hear you because this creates sameness as if having the same experience), a sleep-like state, so that what I say will go deeper into your subconscious mind and this will prove to be one hundred percent successful for you, that feeling of relaxation is wonderful, and we both know how wonderful relaxation feels, as you drift deeper as we continue. You are going to relax into a level of relaxing that you have only ever imagined until now. The mind and body connections are very powerful and as we continue you concentrate on what I say, your mind takes in this information and your body reacts by drifting deeper and deeper into a sleep-like relaxed state. Every time you breathe in, you then breathe out all that past tension as it floats away into the distance; this guarantees your success here today. You are an intelligent person and I know this because you have understood everything that I have educated you with so far today; this also guarantees that you are able to achieve your goal from this moment forwards and you know you are now also achieving relaxation. It may happen slowly at first, each person is different and we all relax at different levels over different periods of time and that is fine. The beauty of this is that it is void of having to do anything, simply relax and let go naturally.

Deepening Trance via Staircase

Now going deeper into relaxation as we continue and you can still hear my voice, and in order to travel deeper into this wonderful sleep-like state, we are going to travel down, all the way down the staircase of relaxation within our powerful minds, this staircase consist of ten steps, see yourself right now at the top on stair ten. This staircase could be anywhere you want it to be, anywhere your imagination takes you, up in the clouds, in the park or anywhere you feel comfortable, like on the beach maybe or even in your own home, as long as you see yourself at the top, on the tenth step of the staircase of relaxation, then the location does not matter as long as you like the location. I am going to count down from ten to one, and as I do, you will imagine yourself stepping down each step with each number that I count down on the staircase of relaxation. For every step you take down, you will drift ten times deeper into relaxation, drifting deeper and deeper into a sleep-like state. And on ten, see yourself stepping, drifting, and floating down, all the way down to step nine going ten times deeper into relaxation with every step you take. Step nine drifting down with your whole body, sinking down, feeling heavier, and heavier as we step down to eight. And on eight, for every breath you breathe in and then out, you are exhaling all the past tensions as we allow you to drift deeper downwards into a sleep-like trance state. Stepping, floating down now to step seven, going ten times deeper into relaxation with every number counted down as we float downwards towards step six. And on six, every muscle in your body relaxing more, and more, getting heavier each and every time you breathe out, stepping down another step to number five. Continue to concentrate on my voice, allow yourself to let go because it feels so nice to relax more than you have for many years. And we continue to go down the staircase of relaxation to step four, feeling wonderful and enjoying this experience as it happens totally naturally, without any effort whatsoever. Step three now, see yourself floating down even further releasing all that past tension as we go, as you relax. In a moment we are going to reach the bottom of the staircase of relaxation, as we drift down to step two, and on one deeply relaxed, your whole body relaxed.

Continue by Deepening Trance Further via Bed Image

Now that we have drifted down the staircase of relaxation, and now at the bottom we can allow your body to relax even more, because I want you to imagine that there is a large comfortable double bed at the bottom of this staircase, where you are now. See yourself walking over to that warm comfortable bed, pulling the covers back and slowly climbing into that safe environment, lying down, pulling that warm blanket over you right now. And as you relax you take one last yawn,(once again yawn so that the client can hear you because this creates sameness as if having the same experience).And that sleep-like state feels warm and safe as we continue further into relaxation. Allow your mind to concentrate only on my voice at all times, as you enter that dreamlike state that feels so wonderful.

Continue by Deepening Trance Further via Body Parts

We are now ready to relax each and every area of your body, and we are going to start with your head area working downwards into relaxation. Each and every muscle in your forehead, right now relaxing, and your cheeks both cheeks relaxing, drifting down, feeling effortless as you continue to relax. Your jaw relaxing and eye lids are getting heavier and heavier, your whole face and head relaxing feeling sleepier, heavier, drifting down, and relaxing. Now moving down towards your neck area, relaxing, your head may drift to one side as you are becoming more and more tired and relaxed. Each and every muscle within your body is going deeper and deeper into a sleep-like state. You will enjoy this relaxed state as we continue, moving down, drifting down to your shoulders, both shoulders feeling limp as they relax even more, you now feel so lethargic, sinking down, feeling heavy as we move down both arms. Allowing them to go limp and drift downwards into a sleep-like state, sinking down into deep relaxation. Concentrate on your chest and stomach area, with each and every breath you breathe out you are sinking further and further down whilst enjoying the experience. Drifting down both arms, relaxing going limp and heavy towards both hands now, imagine all those muscles in each and every finger and both thumbs going limp, heavy and relaxed. (Add your observations of the client's hands and other body parts once mentioned.)

Feeling so tired and relaxed, it is so easy to achieve this relaxed state by simply allowing it to happen naturally and enjoying the relaxation as you breathe in and out relaxing more. Now from the top of your legs, as we work down to your knees achieving relaxation as you drift off feeling calm, safe, and warm. Downwards now, down both legs, relaxing down to your ankles. With every breath you take in, you then breathe out and sink even further down. Imagine your feet, allowing your toes to go limp, both feet limp, relaxed and heavy. All the way from the top of your head, all the way down to your feet, you are now deeply relaxed. And this feeling of relaxation continues as you concentrate on my voice, because what I say is very important to you, because it encourages your subconscious to remember that you are achieving relaxation, and by doing so you will also achieve your goal, for which you came here today.

Continue by Deepening Trance Further if Needed

We are now going to travel into a deeper state of relaxation from the count of ten moving down to one, and drifting ten times deeper, feeling more relaxed with every number heard being counted down. And on ten, drifting, and floating down, all the way down to a deeper state of trance. And on nine going ten times deeper into relaxation with every number being counted down, drifting down with your whole body, sinking down, feeling heavier, and heavier. And on eight, for every breath you breathe in and then out, you are exhaling all the past tensions away as you drift deeper downwards into a sleep-like trance state. Stepping, floating down now going deeper, going ten times deeper into relaxation with every number I count down, as you float downwards towards your desired goal and step seven, relaxing. And on six, every muscle in your body relaxing more and more, getting heavier with each and every breath, breathing out, drifting down towards number five. Continue to concentrate on my voice, allow yourself to let go because it feels so nice to relax more than you have for many years. We continue to count down to four, closer to the level of relaxation needed for success, feeling wonderful and enjoying this experience as it happens, totally naturally, without any effort whatsoever. Three now, I want you to see yourself floating down even further releasing all that past tension as we go, and relax. In a moment you are going to reach the desired level of relaxation as you drift down to number two, and on one deeply relaxed, your whole body relaxed.

Hypnotic Therapy Session Begins and Ends

Dear student, slightly up your tone from monotone to low volume normal speech, then continue:

As you sit, feeling drowsy and relaxed you continue to listen to my voice giving you all the positive suggestions that you require. As we continue you remain in the pleasant state of mind that you are now in. Remaining relaxed and peaceful, even drifting deeper as time goes by. Your whole body developing even further those deep, relaxing, warm feelings from the top of your head to your feet. We are now going to expand upon this new knowledge that you have required here today, making this a permanent part of your new way of thinking. The negative past will simply evaporate like a cloud on a summer's day and a new you will start to emerge for positive effect. My voice may seem to fade into the distance at times, and other times you are fully aware of what I say, this is totally normal as you drift between different levels of trance. Everything I say will seep deep into your subconscious mind, and remain there for your benefit, so that you can act upon the positive suggestions from this day forwards.

Associating Good Feeling to an Anchor

I now want to remember the memory of a time when you felt really good about yourself, we talked about this in the pre-talk when you were telling be about (use information from pre-talk and talk in an excitable positive tone), you feel really happy in that time so see yourself their now, relive it. And when you have that happy, emotional feeling from that past time, I want you to expand upon it, see the situation that you are in, and that wonderful feeling that is generated within you. The content details of the memory are not that important. What is important now for you are the emotional, happy feelings that the memory generates within you.

(Personalise from information previously given from the pre-talk.)

I want you to really remember how you felt inside, those good, positive feelings, and strong feelings, confident and self-assured feelings and the laughter from that time. You can allow those good feelings to grow stronger and more positive whilst you take in a really long, deep breath, in through your nose, and now let's associate that good feeling to pressing together your thumb and the forefinger of the right hand, and by doing so you are making the ring of confidence, so that you are associating that good feeling to making the ring of confidence with your thumb and the forefinger which becomes the anchor. This is an associated emotion to an anchor, when we experience two things together for a little while, one will automatically remind us of the other, and repetition is the mother of success, so keep repeating this exercise over the following days and weeks, so that you are making the anchor of the ring of confidence with your finger and thumb into a signal to your subconscious mind to make you feel good, because that is the happy emotion that is now associated to the ring of confidence. So whenever you take in a really long deep breath through your nose and press together your thumb and the forefinger of the right hand, you are going to feel those good, strong, confident happy feelings once again, and you can feel these good feelings anytime you wish, anywhere, in any situation. Because these good, strong, confident feelings are becoming more and more a part of you and you are becoming that stronger, more confident person that will guarantee your success in achieving your goal of overcoming (whatever the problem was). And remember, anytime you want to feel even more confident, all you need to do is breathe in that really long, deep breath through your nose and press together the thumb and the forefinger of the right hand, and you will once again feel those good, strong, confident feelings filling your whole body in order to make you feel better and better. You can feel wonderful, calmer, more relaxed and much more confident than ever before. You know what it's like to feel those good, strong, confident feelings and you can really enjoy remembering and experiencing those feelings once again, which are becoming more and more a permanent part of you. Feels good doesn't it (suggested command and not a question). Send me a sign that it feels good by raising your right hand (this was using the anchor from pre-talk triggering the right answer). Of course it does because you just created a new more positive reality for yourself, and simply relax and put your right hand down now and that's fantastic. Work on generating good feeling and then press together the thumb and the forefinger over the next few days to reinforce the anchor trigger of good feeling, and see how real that associated anchor triggers the good feeling that can be used in the future whenever you need it. Any time in the future should you have a silly thought towards a past negative problem, simply do as you just have and feel good by saying no to the silly old problem, or use the anchor when in a bad situation to make you feel good, however right now, you can relax and let go of the ring of confidence, because it is not needed at this moment in time.

Improve Confidence Relevant to the Session Type, via a Thermometer to 100% Successful

Now (client's name), imagine a thermometer filled with water, you know what a thermometer looks like and this one has water within it that you can see through the clear glass of the thermometer. It has the numbers one to one hundred percent written on the glass of the thermometer from the bottom to one hundred percent being at the top. This thermometer represents your confidence level from feelings in the past towards your low confidence etc. It may be set at ten percent at the moment; even so we need to achieve a level of one hundred percent for this session to be successful. So let's imagine heating up the water that is within the thermometer with a flame thrower. The water lever is at ten percent at the moment, making your confidence level ten percent, however by heating up the thermometer the percentage level will rise as the water heats up and therefore your confidence level will rise also. By heating up the water your confidence level starts to rise up and up, making your confidence level improve, and rapidly rising 20% 30% 40%. See the level of your confidence rise as you heat up the thermometer with the flamethrower, moving the level up higher and higher, improving your confidence level, and as it does move upwards it is getting closer to one hundred percent, you feel even more confident as the water level and confidence rises. Once the desired level of one hundred percent has been achieved, I want you to send me a sign to confirm that this confidence thermometer is at one hundred percent by raising a finger on the right hand upwards, this indicates to me that we can move on to the next part of this technique. (Wait for the signal then move on). Turn the brightness up in your mind so that you can clearly see the improved overall confidence level, and considering this thermometer is filled with water, and that water is now at one hundred percent representing your achievement made here today, it needs to remain there at one hundred percent. To do this we need to place the thermometer into the fridge freezer. See yourself now; picking up the thermometer and walking over to the freezer, opening the door and placing your confidence level of one hundred percent within the freezer, your confidence level is now frozen forever at one hundred percent and it will remain there forever because it is now frozen. Fantastic, feels good because you have achieved a lot within this session, and you have overcome your past problem, so that your new positive life can start today.

Ego Boost and Good Feeling Story

The following can be said:

Each and every person on this earth, regardless of wealth, looks or ego, all have the same rights to enjoy life. No one is above another regardless of status. We are all the same, and you have a right to be happy, you are a good person, and what one person can achieve, so can another if they so wish. You have told me that you want to (whatever it may be) and the fact is the only thing that has been stopping you in the past, is your lack of understanding and lack of control of your own mind that created negativity. But now all that has changed and this past lack of control and confused understanding of yourself is now part of your past, after all, you now have the knowledge to move forwards in a positive way.

We all get an element of stress in certain situations, and that is normal in some cases but not in others. Even so, in the past it was never the situation that made you feel negative, it was your reaction to the situation from your negative thinking, and you were imagining more negativity, which is just a state of mind. Two people can be in the same situation and one is happy whilst the other feels nervous or sad. So it isn't the situation causing the emotion, it is a person's individual reaction to the situation and not the situation itself. Meaning that it is a person's perception of the reality of the situation, and not the situation itself. You make matters worse for yourself by reacting to your negative thoughts with more negativity, for example, you would say: "I'm bored" or "I feel nervous," and these negative thoughts prolong the negative emotion in the situation and so it gets worse. You must learn to react in a positive way, even if it is an act, because your subconscious mind won't know it's an act and you will feel so much better. If someone puts you down by saying: "You are no good, you can't do that," whatever that may be, then look them in the eye and say: "The only reason I cannot do it yet, is because this is a new thing for me, but I will learn it and then I can do it." By doing that, you have changed a negative situation into a positive one, by reacting differently to it from how you would have in the past. Think positively and your reality will be positive. The past is there for one reason and one reason only, and that it to learn lessons from it, gain knowledge from experiences, and move forwards with the lessons learned. In spite of that fact, you have wrongly been living in the past within your mind, allowing it to effect the present and your future. So it is now time to change, because you want to, and you now understand the "Fright, Fight or Flight Responses." Also you understand that it is your subconscious mind that has been in control at all times time. You now know that all depression and lack of confidence is subconsciously self-inflicted. It is now time to move forwards with your new understanding of yourself, and to take back control. Have you ever thought: "I wish I could have another chance to start over again?" Well this opportunity has come your way here today, so embrace it and enjoy your new beginning. (Client's name), in order to achieve your goal of becoming a confident person, you have to first start the journey towards your goal. Well congratulations, your journey has begun by you making the decision to come here today. You are already several steps up the ladder towards success more than you were this morning. What we need to do now is look at the achievements you have already made in life. You have told me about how you achieved (personalise this part from information from pre-talk), and that time you (whatever it may be). You have brought up two wonderful children, these are achievements that required a level of self believe and confidence, so we know you can achieve whatever goal you set yourself, once you focus your mind on the goal you want.

Let us look at your strengths. You come across to me as a really nice person, and you have told me that you have many friends, people like you and you know this, and you simply need to start believing it, because it is true. You have told me that you are the best at your job (or whatever it may be) and drawing, swimming, looking after children and so forth. These are skills that you have that you are confident in doing due to repetition, therefore we know you already have confidence, you simply need to use it in other areas, where in the past you had felt lack of confidence. You now know that confidence is a state of mind and all confidence, no matter who has it, was once a conscious act that was then taken on by the subconscious as a habit. Confidence must be an act at first, because it is totally natural to feel a sense of anxiety in any new situation, and this is because the subconscious mind protects the person from any potential danger, even though one is not present most of the time. Because of this, in order to overcome anxiety in a new situation, the person has to make a conscious effort to act confident, and by doing so the subconscious mind over time, takes this confidence on has a habit, because the subconscious mind does not know that it was an act, because the subconscious does not know the difference between what is real or imagined, as I explained to you in the mind model, and this benefits you for positive change by acting. You have in the past been focusing on negative thoughts that then affected your mind and body in a negative way. Act confidently and over time your subconscious mind will take it on as a habit, which makes it real for you.

Let us run through that situation that you told me about from the past that you felt anxiety, but this time let us see it with a positive outcome and also add some humour. Let us do that now, remembering you have the ring of confidence that you can use at any given time. Imagine success and that is what you will achieve.

Dear student, talk the client through the story of their experience that they told you about in the pre-talk where they once felt nervous, low confidence etc, and this time instruct the client to see themselves as they would have wanted that past situation to have been. Continue:

That's fantastic. Felt good didn't it? By simply imagining a good outcome, you built up confidence in that situation; your subconscious mind now associates the situation with a feeling of confidence, which overrides the past negative associated thoughts. Later when you are actually in the real situation again, your mind remembers this confident associated link and that is how you will feel, because your mind will remind you of how you felt previously, when you imagined the confident outcome. As I have explained to you, in order to do anything in life you have to first imagine what you want to achieve, this is what you have not done with your confidence level until today, so well done for taking that leap forwards to positive change.

As your confidence builds, now and then, as we all do, you will be confronted with a negative situation or a situation that you wrongly perceive as negative, and so your thought process may make you feel a little down. This is normal, and be that as it may, the difference is that now you will know how to overcome that depressive thought and think positive thoughts, by making the ring of confidence and reacting to the situation differently, by pretending to laugh. Focus on happy thoughts, see how rich your life is, see your achievements and everyday get out of bed with a spring in your step and get things done. You cannot change the past. On the other hand you have changed your reaction to it and moved on and so you have changed your present.

I am now going to tell you a story about a friend of mine called Dave. Dave was one of those guys that people loved to hate because he was always in such a good mood and always had something positive to say. If someone asked him how he was doing he would reply: "Hey, I feel wonderful, on top of the world, life could not be better." He was a natural motivator, and if a colleague was having a bad day, then Dave was there giving them the positive side of the situation. Seeing his style made me curious, so one day I went to him and asked: "Dave, how come you are positive all the time? How do you do it?" Dave replied:

"Each morning I wake up and say to myself, you have two choices today you can choose to be in a good mood or you can choose to be in a bad mood. I choose to be in a good mood, and if something bad happens I can choose to be a victim or I can choose to learn from it. I choose to learn from it. Every time someone comes to me complaining I can accept their complaining or I can point out the positive side of life. I choose the positive side of life." I replied: "Is it really that easy for you?" "Yes it is" Dave said, "Life is all about choices. When you cut away all the junk of everyday situations there is a choice. All you do is choose how to react to any given situation. You choose how people affect your mood by your reaction to what they say and not by what they say. You choose to be in a good mood or a bad mood, and you choose to help others or not help others. The bottom line is: it's your choice how you live your life and what your emotional state is."

I went away and reflected on what Dave had said. Soon after, I moved to another area of town, away from where Dave lived. We lost touch, but I often thought about what he had said when making a choice about life, rather than reacting to it wrongly. Several years later I heard that Dave had been involved in a serious accident, falling some sixty feet whilst rock climbing. After twenty hours of surgery, and a couple of months in intensive care, Dave was released from hospital with rods in his back. I got in touch with Dave some six months after the accident and asked how he was. He smiled and I knew what was coming. He replied: "Hey, I feel wonderful, on top of the world, life could not be better. Do you want to see my scars?" I said: "No thanks," and then I asked him: "What went through your mind as the accident took place?" He responded: "The first thing that went through my mind was the wellbeing of my children, then, as I lay on the ground, I reminded myself I had a choice. I could choose to live or choose to die. I chose to live." "Were you scared?" I asked. Dave continued: "The Paramedics were great, they kept telling me I would be fine, but when they wheeled me into the A&E department and I saw the expressions on the faces of the doctors and nurses, I got really scared, because I saw in their eyes that they were thinking, he's a dead man, and I knew I needed to do something." "So what did you do?" I asked. "Well" he responded, "There was this big nurse who kept asking me questions, and if I was allergic to anything." So I replied: "Yes", and the doctors and nurses stopped working on me, waiting for my answer, so I drew a breath and shouted: "I'm allergic to gravity due to my fall." Over their laughter I told them that I am choosing to live, operate on me as though I am alive, fit and healthy and not dying." Dave lived, thanks to the skill of the doctors, but also because of his amazing attitude. I learned from Dave that every day we have a choice to live happily and fully, and what's great is it is in our control, it is our choice, and we choose our own attitude. So do not think about tomorrow, today should be full enough for you. Anyway, isn't today the tomorrow you worried about yesterday? So from now on each day when you wake, do as Dave does and choose to be happy.

Dear student, this story about Dave I made up just to intrigue the client and to get them thinking positively, the story makes them realise that we all have an emotional choice, regardless of the situation we are in.

How to be Happy and Maintain Happiness

Dear student, I have written this sub-chapter from my own experiences so please adapt from your life experiences. The following can be said in the pre-talk or whilst the client is hypnotised, the choice is yours. I say to the client:

Everyone wants to be happy; it is simply knowing how and maintaining the happiness. Is happiness being in a relationship? Having children? Winning the lottery? The answer is simply, no, because as I have said, two people can have the same things or be in the same situation, but it is the individual's perception that makes them happy and not the situation they are in. In other words, what they have or the situation they are in is irrelevant, it is a person's state of mind that determines a person's happiness or not. By the way, I once won several thousand on the lottery, for all that, it was not the money that made me happy, it is the choices the money brought me, and the choices I made with the money, that made me happy. The win could have easily brought me sadness if I had spent incorrectly, if the wrong choices had been made. You cannot buy happiness because it is not an object, happiness is a state of mind, an attitude to life, and it is what you make happen. The following are the ten golden rules to happiness as I see them:

1) **Reality check**. I have met one of the richest people in Britain and she was so depressed with a totally warped sense of her own reality because she wanted more and more fame and fortune. Her goal was to become famous and she had achieved that. Even so she said to me in a depressed tone: "I want to be more famous." Depression is relative to the person's perception, regardless of wealth or situation. What she needed was to take a step back to see how rich her life was due to the many options she had, which were far more than the average person, due to her extreme wealth. She needed a reality check just as you have needed one here today. Her goal of fame was achievable and had been achieved, mainly due to her wealth and beauty, but it was her only goal in life and so once reached, she was depressed because she wanted that one goal to be more. You need your goals to be realistic and achievable because long-term happiness is gaining pleasure from achieving many realistic goals throughout life and not just having one.

2) **Surround yourself with positive people**. Negative or even nasty, angry people are never happy. It's like a virus eating away at them so that others avoid them. It is a fact that people who care and love others are much happier and live longer than those that don't. I have removed many negative people from my life and I am happier as a direct result. It is far better to invest time and emotions in those that appreciate you and are positive back, than those that serve no purpose. Be a part of a cycle of people that love and cherish, and those special relationships bring joy into your life, as you do to theirs. We all need attention, so best make it positive rather than negative attention, because it is essential for a person's wellbeing.

3) **Show positive affection**. All mammals produce a hormone in the brain called: "Oxytocin." This chemical is produced when falling in love, hugging, kissing, having sex, holding hands with others and therefore it makes us feel good. This hormone is what bonds us to the people in our lives that we love, because it is the pairing hormone that is known as the: "Love Hormone." Once stimulated, it helps us overcome negative emotional problems and it removes free radicals from our bodies. This in turn helps us fight illness, as it creates a better immune system, which also keeps us looking younger.

4) **Be helpful and kind**. Why do people help others, including strangers, when there is no financial reward? Fact is people help others due to the reward of feeling important, of feeling needed and wanted, and it gives us a sense of belonging so that we don't feel alone. We associate pleasure to the feelings generated from being helpful and kind, and that pleasure keeps us healthier and happy and that is our reward. So do something good and helpful for others each day. Be kind, even if it is as simple as holding a door open for a stranger or saying: "Good morning have a good day." You will be greatly rewarded by being helpful and kind.

5) **Laugh often**. Remember that the subconscious does not know the difference between what is real or not. Therefore, if need be, pretend to laugh each day for at least five minutes throughout the day. Look in a mirror and pull faces at yourself, don't take yourself too serious and have fun with it. Walk over to a stranger and say: "I like ice cream" and then just walk away leaving them confused. Do whatever you

need to do in order to amuse yourself and laugh every day. This positivity will become your reality.

6) **Look after your body and mind**. In order to enjoy life you need a fit and healthy body, so for good health you need to look after your body and mind because the two are connected as one. Eat healthy, do regular exercise which means simply move more by going for a walk, and think positive thoughts. Also get plenty of sleep, and if in the past you have not been able to sleep then hypnosis will help, the same as it is doing right now, but on a deeper level. With the help of a hypnotherapy CD that I will provide for you, you can go deeper into trance in your own home and drift off to sleep.

7) **Realise what you have to be grateful for**. Once you get home I want you to write down all the things in your life that make you smile, the things that you are grateful for. Focus on the wonderful things in your life that you already have, maybe your good health, children, parents, friends and family, your job or whatever you appreciate that is already in your life that makes you feel happy. An experiment was done at a University with two different classes of students taking part. The first class was asked each day to write down something that had happened in their lives that they were grateful for. The second class of students were asked to write down each day something that had happened in their lives that they found negative. By the end of the week the first class of students were happier than the second class, they were more positive and optimistic, they looked after themselves more and had less common illnesses such as the common cold, headaches and so forth.

8) **Get out and about in nature**. Being in the country surrounded by nature reduces stress, it is a known fact that mental and psychological health issues are greatly reduced and even eliminated by being in the country breathing in the fresh air. Being in nature allows your mind to wonder and therefore improves creativity. Also it reduces obesity and improves fitness, so that is golden rule six is covered as well. Our minds are relaxed in the country, and watching nature gives us a sense of freedom. After all, we are animals and it is in our nature to want to be out in open, natural spaces.

9) **Do one task at a time and relax**. Learn to relax and that you have already achieved here today and slow down by doing just one task at a time in order to achieve the larger goal. Step back and focus, think about how to achieve a task before jumping in and enjoy whatever it is you are doing. If you are not enjoying it, but the task still has to be done, then it is far better to convince yourself that you are enjoying yourself, because that way the task will be done faster and as a result you can relax more with having more free time.

10) **Forgive the past**. You cannot change the past. However you can change your perception of the past by letting go and forgive those that have wronged you, because they are weak and you are strong. This will help you to positively move forward with your life, instead of dwelling on the past that is of no importance to your present or future. Forgiving the past is the greatest gift you can give to yourself, because it will lead to eliminating the anger from the past, so that you can move forwards in life. Forgiveness removes the pain, the depressive thoughts and anxiety. Move forwards in life in a positive, proud manner because the past is only there to learn from.

Post Hypnotic Suggestion

It is now very helpful and pleasant to go back to the good feeling anchor that we created earlier, by making the ring of confidence once again with your finger and thumb. Make the ring of confidence now, see yourself in that time once again, and realise how good those positive, confident feelings feel right now, those same feelings you felt as it did back then. We have improved your overall way of thinking here today for a positive future from this day forwards. You know that you can use this ring of confidence whenever you chose to, making you feel relaxed and calm around any situation that in the past you had a silly though towards. This wonderful feeling of being relaxed and comfortable is an easy state of mind to achieve, that you can enter whenever you choose to, because we have proven here today that you have relaxed more than you have in many years. You have now placed yourself in a positive reality and that old reality has now gone forever, and this is due to your new understanding of yourself and the past problem. Your goal has been achieved here today and you can now move on with your life, free from that past problem. All this new knowledge that you have learned today, has been stored within your subconscious mind, and this information can, and will, be used whenever you need a reminder to help you through situations that you may find yourself in. All the suggestions your subconscious mind has taken in today are for the greater good for you and the people around you. You will act upon the suggestions you have received because you now know how to succeed, and you know you have, and will, continue to succeed from this day forwards.

We have proven today that you can relax because you have. This is an amazing achievement and a new beginning for you and you can achieve this same success each day. You have learned how powerful your mind is and you know that focusing on positive, imagined thoughts, brings about whatever it is you focused on, in this case relaxation, so well done. Now that you have achieved what you have today, just think what else you can achieve and go and do it. See yourself going out and meeting new people in a confident, powerful way and enjoying it, because you know you are looking forward to doing new things. You are motivated to achieve whatever you want in life.

I am going to give you a hypnotherapy audio CD that you will take home because it will help you relax, as you are doing now here today. You will play it once every day, from today, when you have a moment to yourself, or even in bed tonight and each night. Work on the good feeling anchor every day in the future for the next thirty days, so that it becomes a permanent, positive part of you.

End Session by Waking the Client from Trance

After the count from one to ten, you are going to fully awaken. This process will be slow, giving you time to come around into a fully conscious state in your own time. Once fully awake you will be so grateful and relieved that your past problem has gone. You also realise the amazing positive change within yourself, this has been a positive life changing experience for you. You have not been able to relax for years but yet you have come here today to a total stranger's home, and you have done what you thought impossible, and that is to have relaxed. What you have achieved today is amazing; in many respects it has been a revelation for you. It has been achieved by a simple change in your though processes, it is a state of mind that will now remain with you for life, for continued success.

And 1 – All the suggestions I have given you today will remain with you for life because you now know and understand how beneficial they are to you.

And 2 – From this day and every day in the future, this new beginning for you will fill you with joy of achieving your goal here today.

And 3 – Every morning you will be so happy to have this new beginning free from your past problem.

And 4 – Each day that passes you will get stronger and stronger due to the past problem disappearing into the distance, gone forever.

And 5 – Remembering to work on that good feeling anchor that we have created for positive effect today.

And 6 – All this new knowledge you now have, you can and will adapt it within all aspects of your life.

And 7 – Today you have been able to relax more than you have for many years, proving that you can achieve anything once you focus your mind on your goal.

And 8 – Each and every area of your body feeling refreshed and revitalised, ready to start your new way of life.

And 9 – In your own time, when you feel ready, simply open your eyes remembering all that has been said today.

And 10 – Fully awake now feeling amazing.

Dear student, Give the client a hypnotherapy relaxation CD and tell them they must listen to it every day, or night, as a booster to the session for at least thirty days for added support. This also helps them to work on the anchoring technique.

☐

Your Journey Continues as this Book Ends

DEAR STUDENT, our journey together is close to completion. However the journey never ends, because life is a journey and not a destination, and the same can be said for your growing knowledge. If anyone ever says they know it all, about any subject, then they are very wrong, because there is always more to learn. After years of experience, it took me a further three years to write the first edition of my book: "Beginner to Advanced Practitioner Training Course & Self Development in Psychotherapy - Hypnotherapy - Neuro-Linguistic Programming (NLP) - Cognitive Behavioural Therapy (CBT) Clinical Psychology Vol: 1". Ten years later I am still adding more information, as I also continue to learn from experience, and I continue to share it with you.

I have written four script books. Those being: Phobia - Confidence & Anxiety - Weight Loss – Stop Smoking. You may want to invest in those script books as well.

You may be interested to know that I am working on a series of follow-up books to compliment my "Beginners to Advanced Volume One Book". The next book, which is the second volume, is very different than the first. Allow me to explain:

The entire client examples in all the script books, and in volume one are real, although what I have not done here, or in the first volume book, is write word for word, from beginning to the end, the dialog from full sessions of what my clients and myself have said. Instead, I wrote small sections of sessions from my experiences, to explain techniques to you and how clients think. I also wrote scripts to give you different ideas of what can be said. One of those books you have just read. The scripts were written in a way not intended to be read out to the clients word for word. I simply wanted to show you different, basic beginners and advanced ways of conducting therapy, in a structured session that you can personalise to each client.

In the next series of books starting from volume two onwards, I have written in full detail what is said from recordings that I have made of real client sessions. So the follow-up series, of books, are client case studies with each book being a different client case. In those books I will explain in detail the techniques I am using and why I have said certain things to the client, and I will explain the client's reactions. The client case study sessions were conducted at an advanced level, because that is how I conduct sessions, and therefore those books are for students that have already read volume one, and not just a scripts.

For those wishing to buy the CD's that are mentioned in this book, they are available on one CD Rom for your computer and it has eleven audio hypnotherapy Mp3's with free copyright. This allows you to make copies on CD to sell to your clients to maximise your profits and to help the clients further. They focus on: Stopping Smoking, Losing Weight, Boosting Confidence, Stress Relief, Improving Study Habits, Focus of Concentration, and Pre-talk. Also an induction backing track with subliminal messages of relaxation is on the CD, and that you can play in the back ground as you hypnotise your client.

Simply go to: www.inspiredhypnotherapy.com and then click on the: 'Prices & Online Store' page. You can also contact me through the web site if you wish to have personal training from me.

For those students that have studied this book as a Home Study Course, if you wish to take the Diploma exam, then the option to do so is available as shown on my web site: www.InspiredHypnotherapy.com on the page: "Prices & Online Store". The exam is done in your own free time from the comfort of your own home. You simply email me your answers. Students that pass will receive a Diploma Certificate, as shown on the web site.

Please add me on Facebook – 'David Glenn - Psychotherapy NLP CBT Hypnotherapy'. I am building a community of like-minded people, including my past students. I will post information on my new published books, and we can all help one another with questions and answers regarding psychotherapy as a whole.

Dear student, if you have any questions you want answering to further your knowledge, or you simply want to talk, then please phone me. Phone calls are free via Wi-Fi on WhatsApp from anywhere in the World. Telephone 07973481786

Of course I have to charge for my time. Those charges being £25 for half hour or less. Or £45 for over half an hour to an hour. We can cover many topics in that time. Payment must be made online before the call is made in order to schedule a time and date for our conversation.

I also conduct therapy sessions over the phone if you, or someone you know can't travel to see me in person at the same cost.

Simply email me your details, how much of my time you wish to have, dates and UK times that you are free to talk, and I shall email you a request for payment and set scheduled session. Alternatively in person I charge £95 for a full one and a half hour session.

david.glenn.psychotherapy@gmail.com

Dear student. Can I please ask for a few moments of your time to leave positive feedback on the site where you invested in this book? Without feedback, my time writing will have been wasted, because few people will invest in the book and I simply want to help people to study, to help others, and also for people to overcome their personal psychological problems.

Please note that I am not a professional writer. I am a therapist. Even so, I have done my best to write this book to help others and you. So please excuse the odd grammar error or spelling mistake. This book has been written in UK English and not American-English and for that reason many words are spelt differently to what our American friends are used to.

Thank you!

Dear student, I wish you all the happiness in the world and good health, until our paths cross again in 'Volume One or Two or more' or another script book. Bye for now.